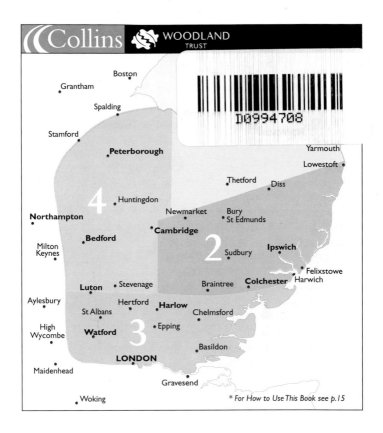

* For How to Use This Book see p.15

Exploring Woodland

East Anglia & North Thames

101 beautiful woods to visit

Collins is an imprint of HarperCollins*Publishers* Ltd.
77–85 Fulham Palace Road
London
W6 8JB

The Collins website address is: www. collins.co.uk

First published in 2002

10 9 8 7 6 5 4 3 2 1

08 07 06 05 04 03 02

ISBN 0 00 714440 7

All photographs supplied by The Woodland Trust. The copyright in the
photographs belongs to the following: Woodland Trust Picture Library 6,
9, 10, 39, 43, 49, 54, 55, 58, 61, 64, 70, 71, 79, 81; Jill Attenborough 8, 41;
David Bradbury 21; Stuart Handley 5, 12, 19, 22, 24, 26, 29, 32, 45, 50, 57,
73, 75, 78, 84; Keith Hugget 4; Archie Miles 7, 66; Helen Parr 68; Nicholas
Spurling 13, 56; Graham Timmins 28; Dick Todd 32. Forestry Commission
11, 30, 31. Ispwich Borough Council 46. Huntingdonshire District
Council 83. National Trust Photographic Library: Ian Shaw 36; Michael
Caldwell 56.

Site entries written by Sheila Ashton, research by Janet Watt
Site maps produced by Belvoir Cartographics & Design

Acknowledgements
This publication has been generously supported by the Ernest Cook
Trust, the Forestry Commission, the Royal Forestry Society and Six
Continents plc.
Exploring Woodland was initiated as a series by the Forestry Trust whose
work is being continued by the Woodland Trust with the intention of pro-
ducing guides for all parts of Britain.

Designed by Liz Bourne
Printed and bound by Printing Express Ltd., Hong Kong

INTRODUCTION

Woodland Trust celebrity supporter, Alistair McGowan, says:
'Can you imagine what our countryside would look like without
trees? Sound like a colourless and dreary place? Woods offer us
peace and tranquillity, inspire our imagination and creativity, and
refresh our souls. A land without trees would be a barren, cold
and impoverished place. When I want to get back in touch with
nature and escape from the hustle and bustle of my daily life, I
love to visit and explore these natural treasures. These places are
rich in wildlife and support a wide variety of animal and plant life.
This excellent series of Woodland Trust guidebooks charts some
of the most spectacular woods across the UK. You will be amazed
and inspired to discover the wide variety of cultural and ecological
history that exists in these special places. Each guide provides you
with the all the information you will ever need.'

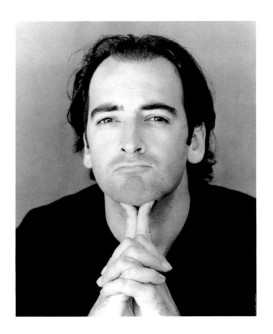

EAST ANGLIA AND NORTH THAMES

A fine spring morning in Hayley Wood, to the south west of Cambridge, is always an uplifting experience. Find an open glade where coppicing has taken place in recent years, sit down with a flask of tea, put your back against a fine straight oak, and soak up the refreshment, not just of the tea, but also the colourful patchwork of springtime flowers bursting forth across the woodland floor. A bluebell blue haze, dotted with white anemones, violets and the gently nodding sulphur yellow stars of the floral show, oxlips. Seemingly a cross between primrose and cowslip (a hybrid of similar appearance does exist) this is actually a rare species in its own right. Now confined to about 100 woods in Suffolk, Essex and Cambridgeshire this beautiful little flower is an indicator of ancient woodland.

Take a stroll around Hayley Wood and you'll find evidence of its former custodians, for a remarkably well preserved woodbank, probably as old as the wood itself, reminds you of the perennial need to protect woodland from grazing beasts. Discover a myste-

Carpet of bluebells at Oldmoor Wood

rious and rare feature within the wood at a strange armed pond, clearly manmade, which is thought might once have been for watering cattle. Sit quietly and who knows you may be lucky enough to hear the sweet song of nightingales.

The very existence of Hayley Wood is frequently documented as far back as the 11th century, and it was clearly a regularly managed woodland producing both timber and coppice wood for a variety of owners down the centuries. Principally oak standards with field maple, ash and hazel coppice, traditional management was renewed in 1962 when the local Wildlife Trust gained ownership of the wood. Sometimes this has proved an uphill battle; witness the deer fences around the wood. Fallow deer have a great liking for trees and flowers and most especially, so it would seem, for oxlips.

As a region it would be difficult to find one containing greater contrasts of woodland cover than East Anglia. To the west lie the counties of Bedfordshire and Hertfordshire, which have long supported dense populations and seen erosion of their woodland in

Primrose

favour of agricultural improvement. Running north to south through the middle of the region lie the counties of Cambridgeshire and Essex, and these, along with the western parts of Suffolk, contain some of the finest and best documented ancient woodland in the whole of Britain. Farther east and heavy clays give way to light sandy soils, more widely planted with conifers, although there are several remarkable enclaves of ancient oaks usually to be found in old parklands.

Bedfordshire lost a large proportion of its ancient woodland during the medieval period when agricultural demands saw it pinned back to the less fertile areas such as the greensand ridge around Woburn. Some woods were under the ownership of abbeys or priories, who derived income from rents or wood sales, whilst others were incorporated into deer parks. Woods reached their commercial peak during the 19th century when the demand for coppice wood was at its height, but by the end of the century, as coal eclipsed wood, their vibrancy declined as many fell out of regular management. Bramingham Wood is one of the most interesting in the county, particularly given its urban location, less than three miles from Luton and surrounded by housing. In this little oasis you can wander through primroses, bluebells and wood anemones, watch nuthatches and tree creepers going about their business or try to spy frogs and smooth newts in the two ponds. In the autumn go on a fungi foray and see if you can identify some of the national rarities which this wood supports.

Eastwards into Cambridgeshire also finds a county largely given over to agriculture, yet it still retains a scattering of small woods (less than one per cent of the land). Many of the county's woods have been particularly well researched, since a remarkable collection of early documents exist which detail their ownership, management and trade. Just over the border lies Bedford Purlieus, famed for a detailed study made in 1975 which identified almost 400 vascular plant species (a record in one wood). What on earth is a purlieu? Of course it's a piece of private land next to a forest, often released from forest laws.

Hayley Wood is an absolute cracker (see below) and always repays a visit. Nearby Gamlingay, also an oak, ash, maple, hazel wood, hides all manner of ancient earthworks, woodbanks and ditches. If you have a yearning to see some elms, or what's left of

Beautiful Hayley Wood

*Hollow tree at
Priestley Wood*

them, get yourself to Knapwell, but don't be depressed by the
apparent decline of Overhall Grove. The rotting carcasses of once
handsome elms take on the appearance of an elephants graveyard –
Dutch elm disease detritus – but hold hard, check the
undergrowth carefully and you'll find young suckers thrusting up
from the root systems. The oak and ash will fair a little better
while the elm overcomes the attentions of the little bark beetles
and the fungus they import. Evolutionary genetics or resistance
will ensure that big elms will make it back to the landscape some
day, meanwhile the dead wood makes grand mansions for bugs of
all kinds and bat roosts, as well as feeding grounds and nesting
sites for birds. The racket of a woodpecker hammering is never far
away here.

The woods of West Suffolk closely resemble those of
Cambridgeshire and one of the jewels in Suffolk's crown is
Bradfield Woods, near Bury St Edmunds, actually comprised two
adjoining woods of Felshamhall and Monkspark. The latter was
once a deer park whilst the former has been a coppice wood since
at least 1252. Bradfield is a species rich woodland in every way,
but this is not just a beautiful place, it is also a working wood, and

it's this ongoing activity which has helped to maintain the biodiversity. Coppice wood is still extracted for making implements such as rakes and brooms, hurdles, turnery, thatching spars, stakes and posts, as well as fuel wood. A little to the east, beyond Stowmarket, lies Priestley Wood. This is another fine example of one of those wonderful remnants of ancient woodland which contains not only giant ash and field maple coppice stools, but also the more unusual hornbeam and small-leaved lime, two trees which become more apparent as you head south into Essex. Wild pear, something of a native rarity and a good ancient woodland indicator grows here, but beware if you find any of the tiny fruits in the autumn as they are mouth wrenchingly sour.

Although the whole of Essex was Royal Forest under the rule of King John, this was only in the old legal sense of forest, meaning a reserve for deer and not necessarily covered by trees. Certainly a large proportion was given over to woodland and fortunately some splendid tracts of that physical forest still survive to this day, manifesting as some of the most extensive areas of woodland in eastern England.

Autumn beech leaves

Hornbeam tree at Hoddesdonpark Wood

Epping Forest, the largest public open space in the London area, has over 2,400ha (6,000 acres) for Londoners (and everyone else besides) to enjoy. However, don't ever take all those magnificent oaks, beeches and hornbeams for granted, for if it hadn't been for a great uprising of public indignation in 1878 the Forest might easily have been lost as a public amenity. The locals petitioned the government of the day in the wake of numerous private landowners quietly partitioning off parts of the Forest, and thus eroding commoner's rights and public access. Their concerns were addressed when an Act of Parliament was passed which entrusted the care of the Forest to the Corporation of the City of London. Until recent years time stood still for the trees of Epping.

Victorian pollards became hugely overgrown – part of the Forest's heritage hung in the balance – vulnerable to either natural decay and demise or a cruel gust of wind. In recent times brave management by the Epping foresters has seen a reintroduction of a pollarding regime. Take a look and see what the Forest might have looked like 150 years ago and more.

Hornbeam is a very distinctive feature of many Essex woods, usually as pollards or coppice stools. Occasionally mistaken for beech, its defining characteristics are a more elongated tooth edged leaf and a grey fluted trunk. Hornbeam timber is the hardest of all native broadleaf species and, although it was once used for such purposes as windmill cogs, its main use seems to have been for fuel wood. Hatfield Forest, famed as one of the finest examples of a wooded forest typical of the Middle Ages, contains many different variations of the hornbeam. Dense compartments of coppiced trees, which would once have been carefully guarded from livestock, are interspersed with open plains of wood pasture, dotted with pollard trees. Some of these pollard hornbeams are outgrown shock-headed trees, whilst others are magical decrepit

Path through Thetford Forest Park

Twisted winter oak at Reffley Wood

veterans sometimes split down the middle so that you can walk right through the tree! Much like Epping, there is also a new pollarding regime in action here.

Swing north to the county of Norfolk and a region of great contrasts emerges. The south west part of the county, largely on lighter sandy soils, contains the second largest forest in England (Kielder, in Northumberland, being the largest). Thetford Forest covers 20,250ha (50,000 acres) of Breckland, and is predominantly a forest of pines – initially Scots pine, but latterly Corsican pine being preferred by the foresters – and there's plenty of heathland. If you're lucky this could be the place to see red squirrels, who live amidst the Scots pine stands, but you'll have to be cautious as they are nothing like as bold as their grey American cousins. The forest is a brilliant open space for families, with play areas for children and miles and miles of trails for belting around on bikes.

If the endless conifer belts do not inspire you, then head north and seek out some of the glorious woods associated with old ancestral parkland. Family fun to be found at Wolterton Park, where there's an adventure playground and an orienteering course or, if you find even the thought of that a bit too exhausting, simply take a saunter along the network of well laid out paths and soak up the mixture of natural woodland and 300 years of tree planting by successive owners. There are some great possibilities for bird lovers here; goldcrests and crossbills in the larch and pine stands, breeding herons and, if you're really lucky, a sighting of ospreys on the fishing lake in autumn. Blickling Woods and Felbrigg Great Wood have a more sedate air about them – the former particularly notable for its fine beeches, whilst huge old oaks and sweet chestnuts feature at Felbrigg.

Autumn colours at Tring Park

Taken as a whole East Anglia is by no means a heavily wooded region, but what is on offer is of remarkable historical and biological significance. Some of these pockets of woodland are virtual time capsules of landscape and habitat which have mostly been swept away over the last 1,000 years. Pick up on the ancient aspects of these sites, compare them to other woods you know which might not immediately seem so interesting, and it will give you an amazing insight into why these woods are so very special.

Understanding and appreciating woodland can really make a difference. Bradfield Woods in Suffolk were under serious threat of clear felling in the 1960s, but because the local populace cherished and understood the importance of these woods they made a stand to save them and were successful. This may not be the appropriate platform to rant from the soap box, but if you are passionate about woods be assured that you have the potential to make a difference.

Where you choose to go and what you want to see is down to you, and this book helps you make an informed decision. Most of the sites are managed to a greater or lesser degree, which means that rather than trying to dive into some tangled thicket you're assured of good access.

Archie Miles

GLOSSARY

Coppice: A tree or shrub which has been cut close to ground level and then grows a crop of branches which can be harvested in future years. Also known as underwood.

Pollard: A tree cut 2–4m (6½–13ft) above ground level producing a crop of branches, out of reach of browsing animals, which can be harvested in subsequent years.

Ancient Woodland: Woodland that dates from before 1600AD. As tree planting was not widely undertaken before that time, it is probable that ancient woodland dates back many thousands of years.

HOW TO USE THIS BOOK

Covering a region that encompasses East Anglia and the area to the north of the River Thames, this book is divided into four areas represented by key maps on pp.16–17, 34–35, 52–53 and 77. In the pages following the key maps, the sites nearest one another are described together (wherever possible) to make planning a day out as rewarding as possible.

For each site entry the name of the nearest town is given, followed by road directions and the grid reference of the site entrance. The area of the site (in hectares (HA) followed by acres) is given next together with the official status of the site where appropriate (see below). The owner, body or organisation responsible for maintaining the site is given next. The following symbols are used to denote information about the site and its facilities.

Type of wood

⬛ Mainly broadleaved woodland
🔺 Mainly coniferous woodland
⬜ Mixed woodland

Car Park

🅟 Parking on site
Ⓟ Parking nearby
🅟 Parking difficult to find

Status

AONB Area of Outstanding Natural Beauty
SSSI Site of Special Scientific Interest

Site Facilities

🔲 Sign at entry
ℹ Information board
♿ Less abled access
🐕 Dogs allowed
⬚ Waymarked trail
🚻 Toilet
⛺ Picnic area
£ Entrance charge
🍴 Refreshments on site

Sandringham Country Park

Dersingham
On the B1440. (TF690287)
243HA (601 ACRES) AONB
Sandringham Estate

A walk through the woodland of Sandringham Country Park is well worth the visit – you might find yourself rewarded with the glimpse of a deer, squirrel, or jay.

Easy car parking and well-laid paths provide good access to the woodland which is dominated by conifers with a few broadleaves breaking the pattern. Some of the trees have been left to mature and just a short walk from the car park you can find some fine examples of majestic looking pines.

Popular at weekends and during the summer, the wood is largely used only by local people on weekdays so this would be a good time for a tranquil walk along one of the waymarked trails of 2.4km (1½ miles) or 4km (2½ miles).

The park itself is well laid out and is a great place to take children, with an adventure playground to keep them amused. Tractor and trailer tours of the country park are provided between the months of April and October.

Reffley Wood

King's Lynn
Reffley Wood lies just to the east of King's Lynn and adjoins, at its southern end, the A149 King's Lynn by-pass road. (TF657223)
53HA (131 ACRES)
The Woodland Trust

Reffley Wood is an ancient woodland site that is gradually being coaxed back to its roots. At present the site is dominated by Scots and Corsican pine and Douglas fir, the restoration programme will re-establish broadleaved woodland, remnants of which can still be found, including a hazel and hawthorn understorey.

In the north east corner a row of old veteran oaks, which once marked the parish boundary, survive and you can see red oaks at the entrance. Many flowers associated with ancient woodland thrive along the wide rides, including bluebells, wild primrose and wild garlic.

Generally the site is flat, well used by dog owners and some paths stay dry while others are particularly wet in winter. Bear in mind that sections of the wood may be closed for management work at certain times of the year.

left:
Reffley Wood

Holt Country Park

Holt
B1149 between Holt and Edgefield.
(TG082376)
42HA (104 ACRES)
North Norfolk District Council

Holt Country Park is also a good spot to take children for a fun day out as it boasts both an adventure playground and a wayfaring course – the family version of orienteering.

Originally planted at the end of the 19th century, the wood was replanted with conifers after the Second World War. Though it's dominated today by conifers you can see birch, oak, beech and sweet chestnut regenerating.

Visit at dusk and there's a very good chance of spotting red, roe and muntjac deer which inhabit the woodland. A spring visit will bring the reward of primroses and meadow saxifrage blooming.

The pond area is popular with visitors and close by there is a tall timber observation tower – tackling it is not for the faint-hearted as you can see right through the slats so a head for heights is needed. But for those who make it to the top there's a wonderful view across the heath and birch woodland that lies to the east.

Sheringham Park

Sheringham

3km (2 miles) south west of Sheringham, access for cars off A148 Cromer to Holt road. (TG139412)

116HA (286 ACRES)

The National Trust

Landscaped by Humphry Repton, Sheringham Park features a woodland garden with rhododendron and azaleas that look spectacular between May and June. You get a great view of them from a special observation tower near the car park.

There's a raised walkway providing some fantastic view points – you can look right over the park to the coast. Ideal for less abled visitors, the boardwalk does however come to an abrupt halt. The more able bodied might prefer going down some steps and slopes into the woodland, which has some large oaks and conifers, and follow through to the parkland where there is an impressive stand of beech trees. The North Norfolk Grand Tour combines a steam train journey on the North Norfolk line with a walk between Weybourne Heath and Sheringham Park. Alternatively you can take a five-mile waymarked route from the car park which leads to the coast.

Old Wood

Sheringham

Part of a larger area of continuous woodland on the higher ground at the southern edge of Sheringham adjoining the Holt Road (A149). A car park is located at the south west corner of the block of woodland. (TG160412)

23HA (57 ACRES) AONB

The Woodland Trust

Though Old Wood, near Sheringham, is currently mainly Corsican pine and Douglas fir, a conservation programme is gradually converting much of the site back to broadleaf woodland and heathland. Eventually it is hoped the heathland will become one of north Norfolk's key conservation habitats – adders and slow-worms have already been attracted to the area.

Visitors should consider 'twinning' Old Wood with Pretty Corner Wood (p.23) nearby. There's a good contrast between the coniferous and broadleaved woodland areas, though both are now being managed for conservation.

While most paths are surfaced and dry, the site is on a slope of medium difficulty, though you can reach higher parts without having to endure long, steep gradients. At the

above:
Old Wood

southern end is one of the highest points in Norfolk with splendid views across the wood to Sheringham and the sea beyond.

West Runton and Beeston Regis Heath

Cromer or Sheringham

A148 between Cromer and Holt.

(TG184414)

46HA (113 ACRES)

The National Trust

Breathtaking views and a fascinating history make compelling reasons to visit West Runton and Beeston Regis Heath. Set near the highest part in Norfolk, the area offers some wonderful coastal views. Earthworks nearby, known as the Roman Camp, are probably where the Romans had a lookout. Shallow pits mark sites where iron ore was smelted before and during the Middle Ages.

The woodland includes sweet chestnut, oak, beech, birch, rowan, Scots pine, sycamore and holly. In the early 20th century much of the area was covered by heather and bracken. When sheep grazing declined the birch, rowan and Scots pine invaded.

Sensitive management is maintaining a varied wildlife habitat. Three species of woodpecker can be found here along with wood warblers, tree pipits and nightjar. There are also foxes, roe and muntjac deer at home here. You might also spot the purple hairstreak butterfly, holly blue, grayling and gatekeeper. Watch out for Adders, which live in the heather along with common lizards and slow worms.

above:
Blickling Hall

Blickling Hall

Aylsham

2.4km (1½miles) north west of Aylsham
on B1354. Signposted off A140 Norwich
to Cromer Road. Follow brown
National Trust signs. (TG176285)

86HA (213 ACRES)

The National Trust

There is a good day out to be
had at Blickling Hall – particularly if you have children who
enjoy a place to run and
explore.

The estate boasts some very
large trees, including oak,
chestnut, beech and pine and
within Great Wood you will
find a spectacular pure stand of
beech trees along a hillside
slope. The best way to reach
them is by using the car park
north west of the estate which
faces them, although the estate
walk will also lead you there.

The open understorey of
beech makes a wonderful play
area for children and the
autumn colours are well worth
a visit.

Paths are well laid out and
clearly waymarked, so it's easy
to really explore Great Wood
and you get good views of the
nearby tower. Other woodland
on the estate is mixed broad
leaves with blocks of conifers.

Felbrigg Great Wood

Cromer
Near Felbrigg village, 2.4km (1½ miles)
south west of Cromer; entrance off
B1436, signposted from A148 and A140.
Follow brown National Trust signs.
(TG195394)
132HA (327 ACRES) SSSI
The National Trust

It's easy to be impressed even
before alighting from your car
on a visit to Felbrigg Great
Wood. Just driving through the
deer park en route for the car
park evokes a real sense of
space and history.

A considered programme of
planting and grazing is helping
to restore this area to
woodland pasture. There are
oak and chestnuts, some
having grown into majestic
trees, with a full form and
shape. Many have suffered in
storms and the gnarled result is
quite artistic. Routes are well
waymarked and the facilities
are good.

The woodland walk takes
you through an area that has
been grazed in the past – look
out for mature trees and grassland with very little else growing underneath, then denser
areas of birch and coniferous
plantations.

Bacton Wood

North Walsham
From North Walsham take B1150
towards Keswick. Turn right towards
Honing. Car park is on right after
Witton Hall. (TG318312)
113HA (279 ACRES)
Forestry Commission

Pretty Corner Wood

Sheringham
From A148 take A1082 towards
Sheringham. Turn right at Pretty
Corner tea gardens car park sign. Car
park is on left. (TG153412)
29HA (72 ACRES) AONB
North Norfolk District Council

above:
Hockering Wood

Hockering Wood

East Dereham

From the A47 go north into village of
Hockering. Take Heath Road out of village. After 400m (¼ mile) take the first
left. The entrance to the wood is on left.
(TG072150)

90HA (222 ACRES) SSSI

Mr M Hutton

Quite neglected until the late-
1950s, when it was acquired by
the Hutton family, Hockering
Wood has a mixed but interesting history.

Used for bomb storage by
the RAF during World War I,
much of the timber in the
wood was felled in the 1920s,
leaving a scattering of oak,
beech, larch, pine and Douglas
fir. But in the late-1950s it was
replanted with larch, Douglas
fir, western red cedar, red oak
and sweet chestnut.

More recently the wood has
been managed for conservation
and ash and hazel have been
reintroduced while thinning of
conifers and broadleaves has
provided some light relief –
and views of some majestic
oaks.

There is a fine stand of 70-
year-old small-leaved limes and
spring visitors can enjoy some
wonderful displays of
primroses, bluebells, wood
anemone, early-purple orchid
and lily-of-the-valley.

Mannington Woods

Aylsham

From A140 go through Aylsham and
follow brown tourist signs to Blickling
NT, which take you onto B1354. From
Blickling, follow brown tourist signs to
Mannington. (TG142321)

40HA (99 ACRES)

Lord Walpole

Top of your 'must see' list on a visit to Mannington Wood is a visit to the unusual arboretum. Far from being a collection of the exotic, it's laid out and planted entirely with native trees. Lord Walpole, who took over the site in 1986, introduced 32 native British broadleaves and three evergreen species, all planted according to type.

The site is well laid out and interpreted, with meadows, wet meadows, follies, woodland and a garden that's renowned for its roses.

Mossymere is the 40ha (99 acre) ancient woodland site, with Scots pine and larch planted in the 1950s and oak, sweet chestnut and hazel. Look out for red, roe and muntjac deer and displays of bluebells, wood anemone, early-purple orchid, white admiral and purple hairstreak butterflies.

There is meadow with a boardwalk, wood pasture with 100-year-old horse chestnuts; coppiced oak, birch, hazel, alder, willow and rowan where you might hear nightingales or spot a tawny owl.

Wolterton Park

Aylsham
Signposted with brown tourist signs from A140 Norwich to Cromer road.
(TG165317)

30HA (74 ACRES)
Lord Walpole

The hall and park of attractive Wolterton Park date back to the 1720s when Thomas Ripley designed them for Horatio Walpole, brother of Britain's first prime minister Sir Robert Walpole.

It was inherited by the present Lord Walpole in 1990 who launched a programme of planting and conservation including organic grazing by Jacob sheep.

Sweet chestnut survives from an avenue near the stables planted in the 1720s and there are London plane and lime along with conifers that were planted in the 1820s. You'll encounter some lovely big beech trees on the approach to the hall and car park.

The park has an orienteering course, adventure playground, spinney with some large oaks, and a fishing lake where osprey can be seen in autumn. Other park inhabitants include barn owls, kestrels, stock doves, sparrowhawks and in the Scots pine and larch, goldcrest and crossbills. Herons breed each year in the upper branches of larch and cormorants live on the island in the lake.

Foxley Wood

Fakenham or Aylsham
On A1067 Fakenham Road take right
turn to Foxley. Entrance is about 800m
(½ mile) past first house on right, out of
village. (TG049229)
180HA (445 ACRES)
Norfolk Wildlife Trust

Norfolk's largest remaining
semi-natural ancient woodland
is the 6,000-year-old Foxley
Wood, a well managed, if
muddy, site that's rich in flora
and wildlife.

The wood was neglected in
the 20th century, as is evident
from the coppiced areas with
oak and hazel standards and
the sections planted with
conifers during the 1960s.

However, the Norfolk
Wildlife Trust is re-establishing
the traditional coppice
methods as part of an active
management programme that
includes thinning, pollarding,
removal of conifers, restoration
of rides and creation of new
waymarked access tracks.

The wood's ancient status is
confirmed by the sight of the

rare small-leaved lime, Midland hawthorn and wild service trees.

Take a walk up the main ride and you're given a striking view of the contrast between the open oak and coppiced trees to your left and the darker, denser conifers populating the site right of the ride.

The rides are rich in flora, including bog stitchwort, bugle, tufted hair-grass, common spotted and greater butterfly orchid, dog's mercury, herb-paris, bluebells, primrose and violets.

Look out for butterflies of the white admiral, comma and speckled wood varieties. You might also spot a barn owl, goldfinch or lesser spotted woodpecker.

There is a circular path around the site with some helpful interpretation points. The main track is surfaced however, boots are a good idea for your visit.

above left and below:
Foxley Wood

27

above:
Autumn oak leaves

Wayland Wood

Watton

Take A1075 signposted to Thetford from Watton. Wood is on left hand side after caravan site. (TL924995)

117HA (289 ACRES)

Norfolk Wildlife Trust

Wayland Wood is a delightful, sensitively managed ancient woodland where the reintroduction of coppicing is already producing results.

The site includes oak, ash, beech and hazel trees and coppicing has opened up space around some of the larger standard trees, revealing some fine oak specimens.

Waymarker posts lead you on the circular route around the wood and there is a clear ride around the site. There's a good variety of flora – including purple orchids, yellow Star-of-Bethlehem, primrose and bluebells and dog's mercury with wood anemone adding colour. The flowering bird cherry in the spring is particularly lovely.

Hevingham Park

Aylsham
A140 south of Hevingham village.
(TG205206)
91HA (225 ACRES)
Forestry Commission

Horsford Wood

Norwich
B1149 north of Horsford village
(TG185175)
84HA (208 ACRES)
Forestry Commission

Snakeshill Wood

Old Costessy
Take A1067 from Norwich and follow
signs to Old Costessy. Go through the
village, past the public house and park
just past the second turning on the left.
(TG158119)
7HA (17 ACRES)
The Woodland Trust

below:
Hockering Wood (p.24)

Thetford Forest Park

Brandon

High Lodge Visitor Centre is signed
from the B1107 Brandon to Thetford
Road. (TL811851)

18,800HA (46,400 ACRES) SSSI

Forestry Commission

Britain's largest lowland pine
forest, Thetford Forest Park is
a great place for a family day
out – and one of those increas-
ingly rare number of places in
England where it's still possible
to spot the red squirrel!

First planted in 1922, the
woodland has evolved into an
active site of timber
production. In the early days
Scots pine dominated the area
and is still retained today,
though it mainly serves as a
habitat for the red squirrel.
The dominant tree now is the
Corsican pine, the main source
of timber production.

That's not to say the woodland is all pines – there are also
areas of broadleaved trees and
more open heathland areas too.

One of the site's strongest

points is its suitability for younger visitors and a family tour of the site can easily stretch to an entire day. An events programme runs throughout the year and there are ample recreation facilities.

The best place to head for if you have young children is High Lodge which is just a stone's throw from one of the 15 car parks and equipped with shop, toilets, cafe and picnic tables as well as some good play areas. Nearby is Squirrel's Maze and giant rabbit and woodpecker play structures which children seem to love.

More adventurous visitors can cycle – on hire bikes if required – along a series of three good trails and even explore a number of bomb craters! There's a small hide at the end of one of the trails, providing a good vantage point for spotting some of the wildlife including the muntjac, roe, fallow and red deer which are resident here. Closer to the centre, there is a bat hibernaculum.

above left:
Thetford Forest Park

left:
Thetford Forest Park

Tyrrel's Wood

Harleston or Hardwick

Situated to east of A140 Norwich to Ipswich trunk road, on Wood Lane. It is 3km (2 miles) south of Long Stratton and 1.5km (1 mile) west of Hardwick. Park in car park at southern end of Tyrrel's Wood. (TM205896)

17HA (42 ACRES) SSSI

The Woodland Trust

Quiet and off the beaten track, and quite isolated in terms of open access

below:
Tyrrel's Wood

woodland, Tyrrel's Wood is a welcome spot for visitors and wildlife alike.

Big Wood, the central section of the site, is an ancient woodland site believed to date back to the Ice Age. It has been designated Site of Special Scientific Interest (SSSI) because of the high variation of woodland types within a small area with particular reference to Plateau Alder Carr which can be found here.

Ancient woodland indicators such as bluebell

and wood melick abound, as does bramble, honeysuckle and briar rose.

Other parts of Tyrrel's are more recent – a new plantation was created in the 1830s but there are oak and hornbeam pollards that seem much older.

Sisland Carr

Norwich

From A146 take turning to Sisland (opposite turn to Loddon). Take first right, and then first right again along track, which leads up to the wood. (TM345993)

12HA (29 ACRES)

The Woodland Trust

Work is in hand at Sisland Carr to reduce the number of conifers, and to replace them with broadleaved trees.

Damage wreaked by the Great Storm of 1987 prompted replanting work which has continued over the last 15 years and broadleaves in this area are now well established.

Nevertheless, the current combination still makes for a pleasant walk through a variety of woodland types. Close dense conifer blocks where pine needles cushion the floors contrast strikingly with broadleaved sections of the wood, particularly in the winter where coppicing has been taking place and in sections where there has been thinning work recently.

Easy-to-follow paths are laid around the site which sits beside a grazed meadow, also part of the Woodland Trust site, which provides a good wet habitat for wildlife.

Three Gates Farm

Beccles

From A143 take road signposted to Aldeby. Access to the site is from Rectory Road – a Woodland Trust sign is visible from the road. (TM456936)

4HA (11 ACRES)

The Woodland Trust

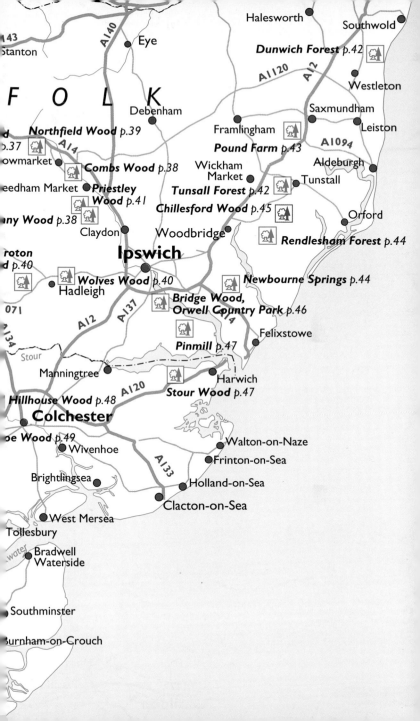

Halesworth

Southwold

Dunwich Forest p.42

Westleton

Eye

A140

A1120

A12

Stanton

143

F O L K

Debenham

Saxmundham

Leiston

Framlingham

Northfield Wood p.39

A14

p.37

owmarket

Combs Wood p.38

Wickham
Market

Pound Farm p.43

A1094

Aldeburgh

Tunstall

**Priestley
Wood** p.41

eedham Market

Tunsall Forest p.42

ony Wood p.38

Claydon

Chillesford Wood p.45

Orford

roton

d p.40

Woodbridge

Rendlesham Forest p.44

Ipswich

Wolves Wood p.40

Newbourne Springs p.44

Hadleigh

071

**Bridge Wood,
Orwell Country Park** p.46

A137

A12

A134

Felixstowe

Stour

Pinmill p.47

Manningtree

A120

Harwich

Hillhouse Wood p.48

Stour Wood p.47

Colchester

oe Wood p.49

Wivenhoe

Walton-on-Naze

Frinton-on-Sea

A133

Brightlingsea

Holland-on-Sea

Clacton-on-Sea

West Mersea

Tollesbury

water

Bradwell
Waterside

Southminster

Burnham-on-Crouch

Ickworth Estate

Bury St Edmunds

5km (3 miles) south west of Bury St Edmunds on west side of A143.

(TL825619)

236HA (583 ACRES)

The National Trust

Prepare for some awesome sights at Ickworth Estate – including some remarkable huge oaks. One is so large that four adults struggle to link hands around the trunk.

Laid out in 1702, this is 'Capability Brown' influenced parkland, with woods, a deer enclosure, vineyard, summer house, canal and lake – and even a church.

Most of the woodland edges the estate, though Albana Wood, an extension of the gardens, feels like an arboretum. It does feature some huge ancient broadleaves and conifers. Look out too for a yew avenue with charming sculptures.

Other woodland belts planted in the 18th century were extended in the 19th century and incorporate Lownde Wood and Dairy Wood, ancient oak woodland.

Great facilities include a living willow play area, deer hide, adventure playground and all terrain pushchairs for hire. Good trails are well laid out but the going can get muddy of the surfaced paths.

left:
Ickworth Estate

Bradfield Woods

Bury St Edmunds
A134 southbound from Bury St
Edmunds. Turn towards Bradfield St
George. (TL935581)
73HA (179 ACRES) SSSI
Suffolk Wildlife Trust

Bradfield Woods, one of the
country's finest coppiced ancient
woods, stands on a spot that has
probably been wooded for 8,000
years.

It's teaming with life – there
are more than 370 species of
flora including dog's mercury,
wild garlic, bluebells, oxlip, herb-
paris, primrose, early-purple
orchid, wood spurge and betony.

The wood has been coppiced
since at least the 13th century
and is a great place to learn about
traditional wood management,
with a working area near the
entrance.

A board at the entrance high-
lights points of interest – the art
sculpture trail is a must.

The tree population includes
oak, ash, small-leaved lime, field
maple, hazel, alder, crab apple
and wild cherry. You might also
spot roe, red, fallow and muntjac
deer – or visit the fishpond bird
hide for a glimpse of a kingfisher.

Paths are surfaced but can get
muddy – so boots are a must.
muddy off the surfaced paths.

Reach Wood

Reach
Leave A14 at Stow-Cum-Quy exit and
follow signs for Stow. Continue on
B1102 and after Swaffham Bulbeck, take
left fork to Reach. (TL565659)
5HA (11 ACRES)
The Woodland Trust

Great and Little Bendysh Wood

Saffron Walden
B1053 from Saffron Walden to Steeple
Bumpstead, turn left to Helions
Bumpstead then left in village to
Olmstead Green. Continue for 3km
(2 miles). Entrance is 400m (¼ mile)
before radio mast on left. (TL627413)
93HA (230 ACRES)
Forestry Commission

Rowney Wood

Saffron Walden
B184 from Saffron Walden towards
Tuxted. Follow signs to Carver
Barrocks main entrance. Entrance to
wood is 200m beyond on the left
(gravel lay by). (TL567344)
69HA (171 ACRES)
Forestry Commission

Bonny Wood

Needham Market

Exit A14 at A140 junction and follow B1078 to Barking from roundabout. (TM076520)

20HA (49 ACRES) SSSI

Suffolk Wildlife Trust

If you're looking for a way to escape the hurly burly of life, visit Bonny Wood. This is classic old woodland, off the beaten track and a trek to reach but also relatively undisturbed.

Records of the wood date back to 1251 and you can sense the history among its oak, ash, field maple and hazel.

Bonny by name and beautiful by nature it's a haven for wildlife, with tawny owls, tree creepers and three native species of woodpecker. Early risers can enjoy a magnificent dawn chorus from nightingales, willow warblers and blackcaps. Or wait for dusk when there's a good chance of spotting deer or hearing the woodcock's mating call.

Coppicing was reintroduced in 1987 and you can already see the results with wider rides, more varied flowers and summer visiting birds.

Between April and June there's a good display of orchids, herb-paris, anemone, woodruff, ramsons and twayblades.

Combs Wood

Stowmarket

From the A1308 take the Combs Road via Combs Ford. Go up the hill and turn left at church. Park at church and follow public footpath onto reserve. (TM054568)

17HA (41 ACRES) SSSI

Suffolk Wildlife Trust

Wherever you look there are pointers to the ancient origins of Combs Wood – in fact the site was probably originally primeval forest.

The area is featured in the Domesday Book – as 'a wood for 16 swine' and certainly there is evidence of its origins on the site, not least the large perimeter banks.

Interestingly, one ride – known as Prospect Avenue – was cut in the 18th century. At that time the wood was connected to Combs Hall by a long forgotten formal garden.

Blankets of flowers along the woodland floor are the result of age and centuries of coppicing. Notable in this plant and animal-rich habitat are the moscatel and greater butterfly orchid, oxlip and wood anemone. Woodland butterflies such as the orange tip and majestic peacock abound among the nectar-rich plants. A typical day in April might result in a chorus of songs from chiff chaff, willow warbler, nightingale and blackcap.

Northfield Wood

Stowmarket

Take exit off A14 signposted to Harleston. From village take road signposted to Onehouse. Wood is on left behind houses (TM023600)

33HA (82 ACRES)

The Woodland Trust

Moves to restore Northfield Wood to its native broadleaved state are already beginning to pay off.

Parts of the wood are already opening up, taking on the look of broadleaved woodland and the wide rides hint at its true status – with lots of beautiful wild flowers associated with ancient woodland including oxlip, ramsons, wood anemone, wood spurge, herb-paris and three or four different orchids. In summer the displays are beautiful, particularly along the ride edges.

Other parts of the site are still coniferous woodland, with the associated 'Christmassy' smells – and the not uncommon sight of deer running through.

The north east side of the wood features two ponds, one of them seasonal, while the north east boundary has pollarded oak and ash trees.

Some of the paths tend to get muddy but the worst sections have been laid with boardwalks.

above:
Northfield Wood

Wolves Wood

Hadleigh

Site is 3km (2 miles) east of Hadleigh
(towards Ipswich) on A1071 on northern side of road. (TM055440)

37HA (91 ACRES) SSSI

RSPB

A lovely example of coppiced
ancient woodland, this Wolves
Wood one of England's
wettest, with 46 ponds – and
consequently a variety of
aquatic wildlife. Wellingtons
essential for most of the year.

Coppicing is being reinstated
in the western part of the
wood and these are the best
places, on a May evening, to
hear some of the 50 species of
birds that breed here regularly,
among them nightingales,
blackcaps, whitethroats, garden
and willow warblers.

In the taller parts of the
wood you might spot tits,
woodpeckers, nuthatches,
spotted flycatchers and if
you're particularly lucky, the
elusive hawfinch.

The woodland – oak, ash,
field maple and hazel – can be
seen from the circular path
which is kept clear and wide
but can get very muddy so it is
not suitable for less abled visitors. But the rides provide a
good show of wild flowers –
yellow archangel, herb-paris
and three types of orchid.

Groton Wood

Hadleigh

Turn off A1141 to Kersey. Turn left in
village past church and head towards
Kersey Tye. Go straight through Kersey
Tye and Groton Wood is on the right
about 800m (½ mile) from village.
(TL 977428)

21HA (52 ACRES) SSSI

Suffolk Wildlife Trust

History-rich Groton Wood is
an ancient woodland noted for
coppiced small-leaved lime in
its northern section, a sign that
this area at least may have
existed since prehistoric times.

The southern part of the site
dates back to the 17th century
and primarily features oak,
hazel, ash and wild cherry,
which is favoured by one elusive resident species – the
hawfinch.

There are no fewer than 22
ponds, most of them seasonal,
where you have a good oppor-
tunity to spy frog, toad and
newt including the great-
crested newt, a protected
species. Flowers to look out
for include the violet
helleborine, woodruff, herb-
paris, bluebell, pignut and the
early-purple orchid which help

bring the wood alive with colour in the spring.

Other notable residents include the dormouse, which makes its home in the hazel coppice and the nightingale – a familiar sound in the summer, along with treecreeper, all three woodpecker species, woodcock and nuthatch.

Priestley Wood

Needham Market
From Needham Market take B1078 towards Barking. Priestley Wood is to the south of this road just before the village of Barking approx 1.5km (1 mile) from Needham Market. (TM080530)
23HA (57 ACRES) SSSI
The Woodland Trust

Considered to be one of the finest woods in Suffolk for its plant life, Priestley Wood is a magnificent ancient woodland site of real historic and floral importance.

A tour of the wood stirs up the feeling of classic ancient woodland, thanks to some signs including woodbanks, boundary pollards and a wonderful rich plant population, and to the wood's history of long, uninterrupted tree cover.

You can encounter several species of orchid, nettle-leaved bellflower, wild garlic, broad-leaved helleborine and primrose.

Centuries of coppicing has produced a mixture of gigantic ancient ash and field maple stools with a sparse canopy of oaks and other trees. Most notable trees to be found here are the small-leaved lime and hornbeam but you can discover the rarest of all native trees – the wild pear, another ancient woodland indicator.

Listen for nightingales which frequent the dense coppice regrowth and also present are sparrowhawk and the secretive woodcock.

above:
Priestley Wood

Tunstall Forest

Aldeburgh
From A12 take B1078 to Tunstall.
Wood can be accessed from this road.
(TM380560)
950HA (2,348 ACRES)
Forestry Commission

Autumn is one of the best times to visit Tunstall Forest with the broadleaves providing a stunning display of autumn colours.

You could easily spend a day here, dividing your time between the huge woodland section and the commons, to discover a good variety of habitats and wildlife.

Many broadleaves line the road and ride edges, with huge blocks of conifers at various stages of thinning in the centre of the wood, providing a variety of light and eerie shade.

There are also some well established broadleaf sections with oak, beech and sweet chestnut and areas of bracken with establishing birch. Some of the area is being kept open and managed as heathland to aid conservation.

Waymarkers and route information isn't easy to come by but anyone with a reasonable sense of direction will find it hard to get lost, thanks to the grid-like network of rides.

Dunwich Forest

Southwold
From A12 take B1122 and then turn left onto B1125. Take northern most road into Dunwich. Car park is on right.
(TM461712; TM468709)
485HA (1,200 ACRES) AONB
Forestry Commission

Visitors to Dunwich Forest can reap the rewards of tackling the three mile marked trail – by discovering a cocktail of habitats, from conifers to established broadleaves, heathland and marsh.

Dunwich has a high proportion of fast-growing conifers. Corsican pine was planted in 1969 and there will soon be some majestic examples. Further down the slope the forest is of Douglas fir.

The nationally rare woodlark has made its home in the forest clearing and the area is being maintained to provide a suitable habitat for the birds.

Broadleaved trees include oak, beech, birch, elm and wild cherry which, when covered with flowers, makes a spectacular sight. The heathland features gorse and bracken and in the wetland area trees like alder and birch are thriving. The wetland also provides a rich habitat for toads, frogs, newts, insects and bats.

A Roman road runs through the south of the forest – it is thought to be one of a network connecting Dunwich with the forts enforcing the Pax Romana.

Pound Farm

Saxmundham

From Framlingham proceed east out of the town on the B1119 towards Saxmundham. Take third turning on right to Great Glemham. Car park can be found on right after approx 200m. (TM325629)

90HA (222 ACRES)

The Woodland Trust

Pound Farm is making an important contribution to replenishing East Anglia's lost heritage of woods, hedges and trees.

Arable farmland until the 1990s, it includes 4.5ha (11 acres) of mature woodland, made up of three small sites. The largest has ash coppice, hazel and field maple with primrose and dog's mercury while smaller areas contain sycamore and some dead elm which has been felled.

Since 1990, 26ha (64 acres) of Pound Farm's 90ha (222 acres) have been planted to create species-rich meadows surrounded by hedges. The rest of the site has been planted with more than 66,000 trees, creating 60ha (148 acres) of new native broadleaved woodland.

Planting is making a real difference – some of the trees are already more than 6m (20ft) tall – the site feels open and welcoming and the meadows are particularly attractive in early summer. Birds are already making their homes here – sparrowhawks can be seen swooping down for field mice and voles in the meadows, where children love to play.

above:
Pound Farm

Newbourne Springs

Woodbridge

Take A12 north towards Woodbridge, at roundabout turn right to Newbourne. In the village turn left at the church and left again following nature reserve signs. Car park is 100m on left. (TM273433)

13HA (32 ACRES) SSSI

Suffolk Wildlife Trust

Newbourne Springs affords a valuable chance to explore a good variety of different habitats within quite a small area.

It takes just 60–90 minutes to cover the site with swamp alder carr, reedbeds and ponds, with drier woodland on slopes that lead to open heathland.

Signs of hazel coppicing, new planting, bird boxes, cleared bracken, new hedges, boardwalks and waymarker posts all bear witness to the fact that this is well cared for woodland.

The route is fairly easy, thanks to a boardwalk on an easy-to-follow path – though less abled visitors should be aware that some boardwalks are narrow and slippery in the wet and some of the paths get muddy.

An information centre in an old pumphouse features helpful displays showing habitats, plants and animals on the site – but it's wise to check for opening times.

Rendlesham Forest

Woodbridge

From A12 take A1152 round Woodbridge. Turn right onto B1084 towards Orford. Rendlesham Forest Centre is approx 6.5km (4 miles) along this road on right. (TM353484)

1,500HA (3,707 ACRES)

Forestry Commission

Rendlesham Forest is well worth a visit, by foot or cycle and, thanks to an events programme and special play area, it's a great for kids.

Take a bike and tackle one of two off-road family cycle trails or take one of the three circular walks designed for various abilities.

The woodland is a mixture of conifer and broadleaved woodland with heathland – very important for conservation – and wetland. Ironically, the diversity of the wood was enhanced by the Great Storm of 1987 which prompted the redesign of the forest.

While there, follow the Phoenix trail through the different forest habitats: conifer plantations of Corsican and

left
*Rendlesham
Forest*

native Scots pine – an important timber source; heathland which supports a whole range of birds (including the threatened woodlark and nightjar, the latter has been adopted as a symbol for the area) and wetland – an important habitat for amphibians and dragonflies.

Chillesford Wood

Woodbridge

From A12 take A1152 around Woodbridge. Turn right onto B1084, once through Butley, wood is on left. (TM378518)

61HA (151 ACRES) AONB SSSI

Forestry Commission

right:
*Bridge Wood,
Orwell Country
Park*

Bridge Wood, Orwell Country Park

Ipswich

Exit A14 at Nacton junction and follow A1189 towards Ipswich. After 200m follow sign to Country Park by turning left. Follow track, go over A14 bridge and turn immediately right to wood car park. (TM187407)

31HA (77 ACRES) AONB SSSI

Ipswich Borough Council

Bridge Wood, in the popular Orwell Country Park is a cocktail of conifers and broadleaved trees, largely dominated by sycamore – and a great place to spot foxes and roe deer.

Especially worthy of note are its beautiful oaks, some dating back more than 400 years, and a veteran chestnut tree. You will notice that some of trees have been pollarded while others – mainly hazel, elm and sycamore – have been coppiced to manage the wood.

A spring or summer visit brings particular rewards. In springtime you'll see a good display of bluebells, wood anemone and moschatel with foxgloves following in summer when you should listen out for woodpeckers, nuthatches and nightingales.

While visiting Bridge Wood it's worth taking a look at the rest of the country park, with a walk by the impressive 1.2km (¾ mile) long Orwell Bridge to the heath and scrublands of Pipers Vale.

Stour Wood

Harwich

Take A210 from Colchester, at Ramsey
roundabout turn left onto A1352. Wood
on right before the crossroads, car park
signposted from A1352. (TM190310)
54HA (134 ACRES) SSSI
The Woodland Trust

Set in the heart of Constable
country – the Stour Estuary –
Stour Wood is a traditional
chestnut coppice woodland.

Records show the wood
dates back to at least 1675
and one of the most interesting things about it is, it's the
only Essex site where woodland leads naturally to
saltmarsh. The saltmarsh,
managed by the RSPB, is a
great place to spot wading
birds.

Chestnut dominates the
wooded sections but you will
find other species including
oak and the rare wild service
tree. Bramble, hazel, birch
and aspen thrive in the shrub
layer.

The wooded sections have
a long history of coppice
management and this has
brought dividends in terms of
the wealth of wildlife found
in the wood – no fewer than
40 species of breeding birds
and 14 species of mammal.

Pinmill

Ipswich

Take B1456 to Chelmondiston. In
village turn left to Pinmill. Car park is
on left. (TM206378)
26HA (64 ACRES)
The National Trust

An unusual route leads visitors
into Pinmill Wood.
Approached via the River
Orwell foreshore, your
approach takes you past old
Thames barges, once important
coastal trading vessels. Then, as
you walk along the bottom end
of the woodland, you can see a
host of boats – many of them
permanent homes – moored
along the estuary.

At high tide, however, the
foreshore path is under water,
so an alternative route –
unsuitable for wheelchair users
– is necessary. This takes you
right out of the car park, 50
metres to steps, at the top of
which is a path to the Hoppit
House where you can enter the
wood itself – Cliff Plantation.

You encounter old alder
coppice, sycamore, elm, ash,
hazel and large oaks. A well
marked and maintained path
provides a pleasant walk, with
steps leading up the steep slope
and the added interest of the
estuary, boats and a pub!

Chalkney Wood

Earls Colne
From A120 take B1024 north towards
Earls Colne. Turn right after approx
3km (2 miles). Turn left at T-junction.
Layby to Essex County Council part of
wood is on right. To access Forestry
Commission section continue along this
road towards Earls Colne and as road
takes sharp bend to left, turn right up
track to car park. (TL869282)
73HA (180 ACRES) SSSI
**Forestry Commission/Essex County
Council**

Chalkney Wood in Essex is a
woodland with something of a
'dual personality', due in part
to the fact that the site has two
owners: Forestry Commission
and Essex County Council.

Spring is a good time to see
the wood, which has a
stunning display of wood
anemones and bluebells – the
Forestry Commission section
the more wild looking. To aid
conservation, a programme of
work is currently restoring the
site to native broadleaved
woodland and coppicing is
being reintroduced in both
sections of the wood.

You will encounter small-
leaved lime, hornbeam, sweet
chestnut and hazel coppice
along with mature oaks,
sycamore, elm and ash.

Hillhouse Wood

West Bergholt
From village of West Bergholt, follow
signs to St Marys, the old church.
(TL945280)
13HA (33 ACRES)
The Woodland Trust

A mosaic of different
woodland types makes
Hillhouse Wood particularly
interesting – and well worth
the trek along the sometimes
boggy track from the nearest car
park on the edge of the village.

For soon after you enter the
wood you encounter delights
like the pond, recently opened
up and a magnet for
dragonflies or, as a result of
hazel coppicing, a seasonal
carpet of bluebells covering the
woodland floor in the spring.

Summer visitors include the
nightingale, blackcap, garden
warbler, sparrowhawk and
hobby while the blackthorn,
found on the ride edge is
favoured by the white lesser
hairstreak butterfly.

The site has undulating terrain – not ideal for less abled
visitors – and this is a wet
woodland with two ponds and
two streams running through,
though volunteers have been
busy creating footbridges and
drying out the path edges.

Markshall Estate

Coggeshall
Follow brown signs on A120 north of
Coggeshall. (TL840252)
809HA (2,000 ACRES)
The Thomas Phillips Price Trust

above:
Hoe Wood

Markshall Estate has all the
ingredients of a great day out,
the highlight of which is its
unique 50ha (120 acre) arboretum which features the amazing
700-year-old 'Park Oak'. This
giant, with a circumference of
8m (26½ft), is the sole surviving
pollarded oak from the site's
days as a deer park.

The landscaped grounds and
park include fine avenues of
oak, lime and horse chestnut (at
the end of which lives a family
of owls), ornamental lakes, the
cascades of Robins Brook and
the recreation of a 17th-century
walled garden.

Beyond the deer park are
nearly 202ha (500 acres) of
woodland – home to fallow
deer, owls, woodpeckers and
sparrowhawks. Mature oak
dominates Bungate Wood while
Crowlands Wood in spring
brings the sight of bluebell carpets and the sound of nightingales.

Visitors should also look out
for the small-leaved lime and
plants such as yellow
pimpernel, woodruff, early-
purple orchid and wood-sorrel,
butterfly orchid, orpine and
herb-paris.

Hoe Wood

Marks Tey
From Colchester take A12 towards
Chelmsford. At Marks Tey, turn off
onto road towards Aldham then turn
left into Tey road by the Big Oak. Hoe
Wood is approx 1.2km (¾ mile) down
Tey road on right. (TL904261)
9HA (22 ACRES)
The Woodland Trust

above:
Broaks Wood

Broaks Wood

Sible Hedingham
Take A131 north from Braintree and then A1017 towards the Hedinghams. The wood is on the right just before the Sible Hedingham sign. (TL784317)
62HA (153 ACRES)
Forestry Commission

Parents of young children seem to love Broaks Wood. No wonder – it's full of short walks, lots of different woodland types and interesting features such as bird hides and ponds.

The main route is clearly marked and well surfaced, if a little on the muddy side in winter, and you can spend a good hour or more taking everything in – including its history. For Broaks is ancient woodland – known as Ruebroche Wood during the 12th century – and there are lots of telltale signs, including 12th and 13th-century pottery sites, woodbanks, rare wild service trees and rich flora.

Owned by the Forestry Commission since 1956 it's now a working wood with conservation a priority. Just into the trail are signs of coppicing of sweet chestnut, hazel and ash trees while other sections are quite dense and dark with conifers.

Brookes Reserve

Halstead or Earls Colne
From A120 east of Braintree, follow signs to Greenstead Green. Wood is 3km north of Stisted on left hand side. (TL816266)
24HA (59 ACRES) SSSI
Essex Wildlife Trust

Named after 18th-century owner Thomas Brookes, Brookes Reserve is a pleasant open grassland site surrounded by ancient coppice woodland.

Once you've found your way around – difficult with no signs and maps – you might encounter a good range of flora – among them dog's mercury, greater butterfly orchids and sweet woodruff.

This is a wet wood with 12 ponds, and keep an eye open for some historic green lanes. Oak is the dominant large tree but you'll also come across small-leaved lime, hornbeam, ash and hazel and this is a great place to witness large-scale coppicing. Once neglected, it has been revived by the Wildlife Trust and charcoal burning is still practised in the wood.

There's a sizeable deer population and a variety of nesting birds – including nuthatches, tree creepers and lesser spotted woodpeckers; visit early spring to fully enjoy the birdsong.

Hatfield Forest

Bishop's Stortford

Exit M11 at junction 8, take A120 towards Braintree. After approx 3km (2 miles) turn right opposite the Green Man public house in Takely Street, signposted to 'Hatfield Forest'. Car park on right. (TL547208; TL546199)

228HA (562 ACRES) SSSI

The National Trust

A popular haunt with family visitors, you get a real sense of history as you explore the well laid out nature trails, walks and impressive open parkland areas of Hatfield Forest.

That's not surprising when you consider this ancient woodland site is a rare surviving example of a medieval royal hunting forest – it was King Henry I who introduced fallow deer here for sport.

The woodland is a cocktail of different habitats – heathland, grassland, ancient woodland and marshland – all of them well managed. And the winding path, which leads through each, provides good access for pushchairs and bikes.

You don't have to venture far from the car park before it leads to an open parkland area where it is difficult not to be impressed by an array of enormous pollarded hornbeams and oaks. Continue on the winding path and it will lead you to a lake, surrounded by heath and marsh, where fishing is permitted.

Phyllis Currie Nature Reserve

Great Leighs or Braintree

Entrance in Dumney lane, Great Leighs. Take road to Felsted from A131 at St Anne's Castle public house. Dumney Lane is first right turning. (TL723182)

4HA (9 ACRES)

Essex Wildlife Trust

Tring Park

Tring
A414 between Runsell Green and
Sindon. (SP 927105)
106HA (261 ACRES) AONB SSSI
The Woodland Trust

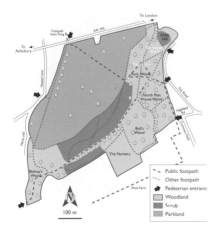

A walk through Tring Park
evokes a sense of the rich history of this unusual parkland,
which is believed to date back
to 1066 and owned a century
ago by the Rothschild family.

Wealthy banker Lionel de
Rothschild bought the estate at
auction in 1972 and his son
Nathaniel – the first Lord
Rothschild – made sweeping
changes to the mansion, and
surrounding farms and
cottages. Lord Rothschild
opened a zoological museum
on the site as a gift to his son
Walter, who was responsible
for introducing numerous
exotic animals to the park.
Wallabies, cassowaries, quaggas
and rheas used to roam the
extensive grassland, which is
still grazed today by rather less

exotic sheep and cattle.

Consequently, Tring Park is an impressive site to explore and great for relaxation, particularly in the attractive open areas dotted with large individual trees and a smattering of new planting.

The woodland is concentrated on the upper slopes where the mixed broadleaves and conifers include ancient beech, ash and yew with scattered sequoias and elegant yew and lime avenues. In its heart is an obelisk, dedicated to Nell Gwynn and the summer house where she is said to have met Charles ll.

A chalk grassland strip sandwiched between grassland and woodland is the second largest area of unimproved chalk grassland in the county and one of Hertfordshire's most important habitats with a rich array of butterflies such as skippers and purple emperor, orchids and plants. In the summer the grassland is alive with lady's bedstraw, yellow rattle, saxifrage and salad burnet. The Woodland Trust is managing the grassland through a programme of scrub control.

King Charles Ride, a long distance footpath, runs through the site and provides some wonderful views across the Chilterns. The Ridgeway National Trail is being redirected along the bridleway along the top of the scarp.

above left:
Tring Park

below:
Tring Park

Ashridge

Berkhamstead
Take A4251 towards Tring, turn right at
Northchurch onto B4506 to Ashridge.
Visitor centre and monument car park
on left. (SP 971131)
2,000HA (4,942 ACRES) AONB SSSI
The National Trust

Great views, good for children
and some magnificent looking
trees – just three reasons to
visit the Ashridge estate in the
Chiltern Hills.

below: *Ashridge*

Covering 15.5 km² (6 sq.
miles) of land between
Berkhamsted and Ivinghoe
Beacon, it features woods,
common land and chalk down-
land, with good car parking. A
number of vantage points offer
splendid views across the estate,
including Ivinghoe Beacon – a
little walk away but well worth
it. Steps also lead to a large
monument, dating back to 1832,
which is open April to October
at weekends and bank holidays.

Some impressive old trees
can be found in the open
woods, which features oak,
beech and ash. The paths are
wide and firm, occasionally
surfaced and provide access
from the monument into the
surrounding woodland and
open commons.

Popular with parents of
young children and dog owners,
the site has a visitor centre open
daily April to October.

Sherrardspark Wood

Welwyn Garden City
Exit A1(M) at junction 6 and take
B1975 to Stanborough. Turn left imme-
diately before railway bridge on
Rectory Lane. Car park is on right after
reservoir buildings. (TL228140)
81HA (200 ACRES) SSSI
Welwyn Hatfield Council

North Cycleway, providing good access. Coppicing has been reintroduced in this western section of the wood.

Look out for some very tame squirrels or the odd muntjac deer or fox. The woodland is also home to three species of woodpecker, tawny owl, jay, sparrowhawk and hawfinch.

Mardley Heath

Knebworth

Take B197 towards Knebworth. Once over railway bridge, just south of Woolmer Green, turn left on Heath Road. Car Park is on right. (TL249184)
42HA (104 ACRES)
Welwyn Hatfield Council

Watling Chase Community Forest

The Watling Chase Community Forest aims to create an attractive landscape, where woodland and hedgerows will form a mosaic with other land uses, by working in partnership with public and private enterprises, farmers, landowners, voluntary groups, schools, colleges and local people. The aim is to improve the environment for people and wildlife and to provide new opportunities.

above:
Sherrardspark Wood

A spacious and undulating woodland with some enormous oaks, Sherrardspark Wood is widely regarded as one of Britain's finest sessile oak and hornbeam woods. It was originally called 'Sheregge in Dychenswell' meaning 'bright ridge'. It is suggested this refers to the white chalk that comes to the surface in the north of the wood.

Spring visitors can enjoy a wonderful display of bluebells and anemone or blooming rhododendrons along the main ride through May and June.

Access is good, thanks to clearly marked paths and a disused railway line that dissects the western section of the wood and was recently resurfaced to form part of the Great

left:
Harrocks Wood

Harrocks Wood

Chandler's Cross

From A41 travelling south towards Watford, turn right at church and traffic lights in Hunton Bridge. Once in Chandler's Cross, turn left onto Rousebarn Lane. (TQ066977)

45HA (110 ACRES)

The Woodland Trust

Five woods for the 'price' of one is your reward for a visit to Harrocks Wood. It is inter-linked with four other sites – Whipendell Wood (managed by the local authority), Merlin's Wood, Dell Wood and Newland's Spring (managed by the Woodland Trust) – via a series of footpaths. A tour of all five provides a pleasant contrast between woodland and open farmland.

Birch and sycamore abound – the legacy of a programme of felling the larger mature beech, oak and ash trees prompted since the estate was broken up and sold 100 years ago.

Spring brings a fantastic display of bluebells, though dog's mercury is more common in Newland's Spring and some of Dell Wood. Look out too for celandine and primrose. Later in the year you can see speedwells and campions along with the more unusual coralroot bitter-cress.

A programme of coppicing and opening up the paths has resulted in an abundance of butterflies, including the red admiral. And it's not uncommon to spot muntjac and fallow deer.

Ruislip Woods

Ruislip

From Ruislip tube take A4180 to main roundabout, fork left (still on A4180) and turn right into Reservoir road. Lido

is on right. (TQ 086890)

305HA (750 ACRES) SSSI

London Borough of Hillingdon

The Ruislip woods complex is one of the largest areas of ancient woodland in London, with some parts dating back to the Wildwood which covered England after the last ice age about 8,000 years ago. Public outcry saved these valuable woods from development in the 1930s and in 1997 they were designated as the first National Nature reserve in London. The woods are well served by public transport, have good car parks and a horse-riding circuit. The trees themselves are mainly coppiced hornbeam with oak standards.

The site includes a lido and there is a pub near the main entrance.

Gutteridge and Ten Acre Woods

Uxbridge

Turn off A40 on A437 to Hillingdon. Turn left on Ryefield Avenue and left onto Berkley Road. Park at end of road on Lynhurst Crescent. (TQ086843; TQ097836)

36HA (89 ACRES)

London Borough of Hillingdon

Big oak trees and a dense understorey, ablaze with a blanket of bluebells in spring, help to make Gutteridge Wood a delight to visit, with the 'feel' of an old natural and wild wood.

Hazel coppicing is still being carried out in the wood and the meadows that surround it produce colourful displays of wild flowers in the spring, and crackle with the sounds of crickets and grasshoppers. The south east section of the wood makes a great picnic spot when the weather is dry. Keep your eyes open for a glimpse of kingfishers along the brook.

A narrow, muddy path crosses the neighbouring fields and links to Ten Acre Wood, a 100-year-old oak plantation with lots of hawthorn and blackthorn. During the early part of the year it sustains some beautiful blossoms, followed by a good supply of berries to nurture birds during the autumn and winter.

Berrygrove Woods

Watford, Radlett or Bushey

From Radlett take B462 for approx 5km (3 miles) which takes you to the entrance by M1 bridge. (TQ134979)

405HA (1,000 ACRES)

Hertfordshire County Council

Fryent Country Park

Wembley or Harrow
Fryent Way on A4140. (TQ196876)
100HA (247 ACRES)
Brent Council

Deep in the heart of London suburbia lies a wonderful woodland idyll.

Fryent Country Park is a wonderful mix of organically managed open grassland, hay meadows with more than 200 species of wild flowers that teem with butterflies, wonderful old hedgerows dotted with imposing mature trees – and 27 ponds, 15 of them new. It's a pity Fryent Way – a busy road – bisects the park but Gotfords Hill offers a good view across the park and beyond.

Woodland crowns the summit of Barn Hill which provides commanding views over some of London's landmarks. The woodland includes oak, ash, hornbeam, beech, sweet chestnut and elm planted by Humphry Repton in 1783 and a 1930s Lombardy poplar avenue gives Barn Hill a distinctive skyline. Scrub developing rapidly on the hilltop is being managed to encourage the grassland habitat.

Four new woods have been planted since the 1980s – Beane Hill, Lower Hydes, Eastlands and Summers Croft, while a former orchard is being re-established alongside a newly planted cobnut plantation.

Highgate Wood

Camden Town or Highgate
Site runs to the west of B550 Muswell Hill Road. (TQ280883)
28HA (70 ACRES)
Corporation of London

What does the rare golden oriole have in common with the sparrowhawk, 180 species of moth and 80 species of spider?

They all inhabit the ancient woodland site of Highgate Wood which once formed part of the Forest of Middlesex featured in the Domesday Book.

Breeding foxes, five species of bat, fungi which flourishes in the dead wood among the oak, hornbeam and the rare wild service tree are all to be found here, making for an extremely rich experience as you walk through the wood.

Highgate Wood 'feels' old yet it's obviously well managed and cared for. Parts of the wood have been fenced off to aid regeneration of the trees and encourage wild flowers like the bluebell and wood anemone.

There's an excellent information centre, jam-packed with information and exhibits, and playground and playing field facilities to keep the children happy, along with a specially designed woodpecker trail. Adults, meanwhile, might prefer the mile-long history trail.

Hampstead Heath

Camden Town and Hampstead
Signposted from A502. (TQ260865)
320HA (791 ACRES) SSSI
Corporation of London

Who could be surprised that Hampstead Heath is a people magnet? This vast open space in the very heart of London has everything – from children's playgrounds to a wildlife garden and a very good information centre.

But despite all the activity that goes on year-round on the site, you can still make your way into the woods and lose yourself among those huge oak trees where birds like sparrowhawks, fieldfares, redwings, kestrels, tawny owls and woodpeckers make their homes. At dusk you could spot one of at least five species of bat the wood supports while some 25 ponds provide habitats for newts, frogs and toads and a multitude of wildfowl. Hampstead Heath attained Site of Special Scientific Interest (SSSI) status due to the richness of flora and fauna found here.

Children are spoiled for choice with an under fives' centre, traditional playground and paddling pool, interactive displays in the information centre at Parliament Hill Lido and a vast choice of activities, from concerts at Kenwood to sports pitches, and open air swimming. Not to mention some stunning views of the capital. Exhausting? It's worth it!

below:
Wormley and Nut Wood (see p.62)

Wormley and Nut Woods

Hoddesdon

From the A10, follow brown signs to the Paradise Wildlife Park. Continue past the Park on White Stubbs Lane and also past the Bencroft East car park. Park in Bencroft West car park which is on the left hand side. (TL326062)

143HA (353 ACRES) SSSI

The Woodland Trust

High on the list of 'must see' woods is Wormley and Nut Woods – a National Nature Reserve – with its vast expanse of ancient woodland populated by huge old oaks that actually 'feels' centuries old.

Wormley Wood is mentioned in 6th-century documents about Ermine Street, which runs east of the wood, and is noted for its birds – hawfinch, redstart and woodpeckers among them – and its fungi, mosses and ferns, flourishing by the woodland ponds and streams.

Traditionally coppiced for more than 300 years Wormley had lost around a third of its oak and hornbeams to conifer plantation by the early 1980s. Restoration work has begun, however and conifers are being removed, allowing regeneration of sessile oak, ash,

hornbeam and aspen. It's easier to get around, thanks to restoration work on paths. Plants abound – including sweet woodruff, yellow archangel, dog's mercury, bluebell displays in the spring and the beautifully scented honeysuckle in the summer.

Interesting features include a circular sculpted seat encircling a tree, and a 17th-century coalpost.

Northaw Great Wood

Cuffley

Exit M25 at junction 24 and get onto A1000 towards Potters Bar. Turn right onto B157, Shepherds Way, and then left on The Ridgeway, signposted to Cuffley and Cheshunt. Wood is on left. (TL281039)

121HA (300 ACRES) SSSI

Welwyn Hatfield Council

Until 1806, Northaw Great Wood was common land, with coppiced and pollarded hornbeam and sweet chestnut.

Today it's a mixture, with oak, birch and areas of ash and sycamore, including two very large, impressive beech trees encountered on one of the three waymarked trails.

A horse trail runs through the wood, which occupies an undulating – occasionally steep

– site with a stream and a good variety of flora and wildlife.

Look out for muntjac deer, foxes and badgers and a varied bird population including nightingales, warblers, woodpeckers, tawny owls and migrant siskin and woodcock. Colour is provided by the dog's mercury, bluebells and wood anemone that grow in the woodland. By the stream you might discover lesser celandine, wood sanicle, ragged robin and bugle.

Paths are provided but it's a muddy wood so it's sensible to go equipped with boots or wellingtons.

Danbury Common

Danbury

Off the A414 road from Chelmsford to Maldon. (TL281044)

86HA (211 ACRES) SSSI

The National Trust

What makes Danbury Common so interesting is the large variety of different and contrasting wildlife habitats you discover in a relatively small area.

A waymarked route leads you through most of the different sections: heathland in the middle, coppiced woodland on the edge and

north east of the site grassland and some new woodland.

The wood has quite an open feel, although there are quite a few areas of dense scrub woodland that are virtually impenetrable, especially where blackthorn is growing. The commons had been grazed until the early part of the 20th century. When this stopped, scrub developed at the expense of the heather and grassland.

Other parts of the site have more developed woodland and here you will find birch, oak, hazel, hornbeam and ash.

It's a good site for families too, with a large open area by the car park that is ideal for picnics or family activities such as kite-flying.

Thunderfield Grove

Hoddesdon

Take B198 towards Goff's Oak, turn right onto B156, turn left onto a minor road after 1 mile. Turn 1st right towards Flamstead End, after nearly a mile turn right into Park Lane Paradise. Thunderfield Grove is on left after 800m (½ mile). (TL338052)

25HA (61 ACRES)

The Woodland Trust

left:
*Hoddesdonpark
Wood*

Hoddesdonpark Wood

Hoddesdon

From Hertford and A1, take A414
towards Hertford Heath from town
centre. Follow signs for Balls Park. This
minor road runs southwards for 5km
(3 miles) to Goose Green. Wood is on
Lord Street on right. (TL348088)
62HA (154 ACRES) SSSI
The Woodland Trust

Hoddesdonpark is a delightful
oak-hornbeam wood with a
decidedly majestic feel, due
largely to the grandness of its
numerous tall, straight mature
oaks and wide rides.

It makes a delightful combination with the beautiful
hornbeam with its twisted
branches and smooth, grey
trunks. Visit the site in
summer and you'll notice the
heady scent of the
honeysuckle covering many of
the trees – a great draw for the
white admiral butterfly.

Follow the waymarked trail
and you get a feel for the
space and size of the wood,
yet still a sense of intimacy as
you walk along the narrower

winding paths, the first of which leads to one of two ponds that can be found in the wood, along with numerous streams.

There's a strong sense of history here, too. Woodbanks, believed to date back to the Middle Ages, can be found on three sides of the wood which was coppiced until the 19th century.

Broxbourne and Bencroft Woods

Hoddesdon

6.5km (4 miles) south of Hertford. From Hoddesdon, follow Cock Lane from A1170 at roundabout near Civic Centre for just over 3km (2 miles). (TL327069; TL326065)

55HA (135 ACRES) SSSI

Hertfordshire County Council

A large deer population has led to some artistic touches in the coppiced parts of Broxbourne and Bencroft Woods where some intricate hurdles and basket work has been created to deter the animals from grazing.

The woods form part of the Broxbourne Woods National Nature Reserve, with the Woodland Trust's Wormley and Nut Woods and

Hoddesdon Park Wood making up the remainder.

The woodland is a mixture of hornbeam coppice, oak, birch, ash, wild cherry and alder and there are also blocks of 1960s conifers, especially in Broxbourne.

Varied and well managed, the woods boast streams, ponds and a wildlife population that includes badgers and grass snakes, birdlife including woodpeckers, tree creepers, sparrowhawks, woodcocks and buzzards while butterflies such as orange tip, skipper and speckled wood add to the pleasure of a visit.

A series of trails has been planned out in the wood but to access these you are likely to need the map from the owner.

Post Wood

Ware or Hertford

Exit A10 and get onto A1170 to Ware. In Great Amwell, turn left onto Post Wood road. Park on roadside at top. (TL362134)

10HA (24 ACRES)

East Herts District Council

Epping Forest

Loughton

Exit M25 at junction 26 or M11 at junction 5 and follow signs to Epping Forest. (TQ412938)

2,300HA (5,685 ACRES) SSSI

Corporation of London

It is possible to spend an entire day in the countryside without leaving London – by exploring Epping Forest – at 2,300ha (5,685 acres), the largest public open space in London. Two thirds is wooded with the same proportion having Site of Special Scientific Interest (SSSI) status.

Epping Forest dates back thousands of years, although the woods you will see today are a

top left:
Epping Forest

Key:

- Epping Forest boundary
- Car park
- Epping Forest Information Centre
- Viewpoint

1 Copt Hall Green
2 Ambresbury Banks
3 The Ditches
4 Wake Valley Pond
5 Great Monk Wood
6 High Beach
7 Loughton Camp
8 Fairmead Bottom
9 Gilwell Park
10 Chingford Water
11 Connaught Water
12 Queen Elizabeth's Hunting Lodge
13 Pole Hill
14 Knighton Wood

'mere' 1,500 years old. Once turned into a royal hunting ground by the Normans, large parts of the site were earmarked for development in the 19th century. But public concern led, in 1878, to its ownership being transferred to the City of London.

The rich history of Epping Forest is matched by an abundance of wildlife, including three different woodpecker species, nightingales and nuthatches. Scores of artificial ponds and lakes attract waterfowl, great crested grebes and goosander and it's possible to find 650 different plant species including 50 types of trees and shrubs. Oak, birch, beech and hornbeam dominate – some trees are spectacularly large and some strangely misshapen as they are pollards.

It hosts a variety of activities and encompasses the Grade II listed Wanstead Park, two historic listed buildings – Queen Elizabeth's Hunting Lodge and the Temple – and the remains of two large Iron Age earthworks.

Epping Forest Information Centre at High Beech houses exhibitions exploring the history of the forest and its inhabitants, has a wide range of books and leaflets and runs a regular programme of guided walks.

above:
Swan Wood and Cygnet Wood

Swan Wood and Cygnet Wood

Billericay

From Chelmsford take the B1007 south towards Billericay. In Stock turn right into Swan Lane, Swan Wood is on the right after 400m (¼ mile), park on left. (TQ688993)

21HA (52 ACRES)

The Woodland Trust

Old blends attractively with new at Swan Wood and its appropriately named neighbour, Cygnet Wood.

Swan Wood is an ancient woodland site, with slopes and streams where coppicing and pollarding of the trees has given the area a distinctive character.

The wood has been extended all around and on one side the Woodland Trust has planted a 'Woods on Your Doorstep'

site. A section (Cygnet Wood) is being left to colonise naturally from Swan Wood.

Bluebells that burst into delightful colour in May bear testimony to the fact that Swan Wood is ancient and there's more evidence in the form of internal woodbanks and remnants of its medieval boundary which can still be seen – one section is just a few metres in from the entrance.

Next to the wood is meadow that has been left as open pasture and is grazed by horses. Work is also being carried out to restore an old pond.

Gernon Bushes

Epping

Exit M7 at junction 11 and take B1393 towards Epping. Turn left on B181. Then take first right signposted to Coopersale village. Pass under railway bridge and take immediate left, Gardon Mead. Entrance to wood is on left. (TL478030)

32HA (79 ACRES) SSSI

Essex Wildlife Trust

One of the striking sights at Gernon Bushes are the amazing hornbeam pollards, beautiful, twisting gnarled old trees with smooth bark that can take on an eerie air in misty weather. You'll see the full effect by following the bridleway to the left at the end of Garnon Mead.

It's a well-managed site – much of it served by a surfaced track – and boardwalks are provided in the muddier sections.

Much of the wood has an open feel to it, with wide rides cutting between oak and hornbeams.

There are quite a few ponds in the wood and springs which descend down steep-sided valleys to form bogs with patches of rare marsh fern. Other species to look out for include lady fern, bog bean, marsh valerian, kingcup and ragged robin. And don't forget to keep your eyes and ears open for the hawfinch and sparrowhawks which are regular visitors.

Langdon Reserve

Laindon

From A127 take B148. At traffic lights turn immediately right, signed Horndon-on-the-Hill. Pass under railway bridge and conservation centre is signed on left. (TQ659874)

184HA (458 ACRES)

Essex Wildlife Trust

Comprising 184ha (458 acres) of meadows, woods, ponds, plantations, scrub and former Plotland gardens, Langdon Reserve offers lots to see and a good events programme.

Worth exploring are the plant-rich Plotlands, including a furnished 1930s Plotland bungalow. These little pieces of countryside were auctioned off in small plots in the early 1900s to people, mainly from the east end of London, after the agricultural depression of the 1890s.

The surrounding scrubland and ancient woodland – Lincewood and Marks Hill – is bustling with colour and wildlife, including nightingales and warblers, bluebells and primroses, adder, lizards, butterflies and old roses.

Coppicing has been re-introduced at Marks Hill, while the former deer park, Willow Park is 90ha (220 acres) of hay meadow, with ancient hedgerows, large ponds and an ancient hornbeam wood called Longwood.

The Old Park

Brentwood

Take A128 towards Ingrave. After railway crossing turn right, follow signs north to Thorndon Country Park. After approx 1.5km (1 mile) turn left and drive to second County Council car park. (TQ618906)

55HA (135 ACRES)

The Woodland Trust

Hainault Forest

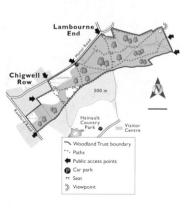

Woodland Trust boundary
Paths
Public access points
Car park
Seat
Viewpoint

Chigwell

From A1112 towards Chigwell Row, continue past signs to Hainault Country Park visitor centre. Turn right into Manor Road near Church. Car park is on right. (TQ475935)

129HA (319 ACRES) SSSI

The Woodland Trust

Grand in size, stature and origins, Hainault Forest today is, in fact, just a tiny remnant of what was once the 'Forest of Essex.' Nevertheless, this is a site of national historic, cultural and landscape importance.

A former royal hunting forest and created to provide venison for the King's table, it's one of the best surviving medieval forests of its kind, dominated by the distinctive top heavy and distorted shapes of veteran hornbeam pollards which the Woodland Trust is working hard to revitalise.

It's estimated Hainault has around 6,000 veteran Hornbeam pollards, numerous large oaks and a few ash pollards, all supporting myriad species, from owls, woodpeckers and bats to whole communities of specialised insects, lichens, mosses and fungi.

Hainault has rather fewer plant species than similar woods of comparable size, however, bramble, holly and hazel are all in evidence.

Hainault's status as an ancient woodland is confirmed in spring when dense carpets of bluebells make a stunning sight between April and June. The rare wild service tree and

butcher's broom (once prized as a scrubbing brush for butchers' blocks) also provide strong evidence of its age.

Another notable feature of Hainault is a small area of heather heathland – rare in Essex – where key plants such as dwarf gorse and lousewort have been recorded. There is also a pond next to which, it's believed a local herbalist called Dido lived in the 19th century, producing alternative medicines from the forest trees and plants.

above left:
Hainault Forest

right:
Hainault Forest

Norsey Wood

Billericay

From Billericay take A129 to Wickford.
Turn left on Outwood Common road.
Follow road past church, turn right at
mini roundabout to remain on Outer
Common road. Go over railway line,
wood and car park on left. (TQ691956)
71HA (175 ACRES) SSSI
Basildon District Council

Norsey Wood is a great wood
to explore whether you're
young or old, able bodied or
less able, thanks to some excellent trails (don't forget your
information leaflet) and a fascinating history.

The 67ha (165 acre) ancient
woodland site has coppiced
sweet chestnut, oak and hornbeam, and wetter areas with alder
carr, ash and willow. The wood
has been coppiced for 1,000 years
and still has a working woodyard
where you can buy wood prod-
ucts on weekend mornings.

This is a wet wood, with
ponds and a stream and in the
south there is a stand of larch.
The coppicing has brought bene-
fits for flora such as stitchwort,
violet and St John's wort while
blackcaps and wrens also benefit.

Bluebells, wood anemone
and lily-of-the-valley are all
present. There is also a good
butterfly population.

Danbury Ridge Reserves

Danbury

From A12 to east of Chelmsford, take
A414 towards Maldon. In Danbury
turn left at Eve's Corner along Little
Baddow Road. After 600m (⅓ mile) turn
right onto Runsell Lane. Park on roadside. (TL775064)
101HA (250 ACRES) SSSI
Essex Wildlife Trust

A trail takes you neatly
through a mosaic of woodland,
common and heathland,
streams, bogs and farmland
that makes up the Danbury
Ridge Reserves.

Coppicing is being reintroduced and maintenance work
includes bog restoration and
scrub clearance.

Dormice live in many parts
of the reserve while the bird
population features nuthatch,
hawfinch, nightingale and
three types of woodpecker.
Brimstone, ringlet and small
copper butterflies also thrive
here.

Woodham Walter Common
is secondary woodland, noted
for its sessile oaks while rowan
features strongly with a
scattering of wild service trees
and alder buckthorn.
Hornbeam coppice dominates
Birch Wood, ablaze in spring

above:
Danbury Ridge

with wood anemones, wood spurge, wood-sorrel and white climbing fumitory.

Acres of lily-of-the-valley grow in Pheasanthouse Wood, a mixed site with three raised bogs, dense sphagnum moss, the rare lesser skullcap and smooth and star sedges. Other areas include oak pollards of Poors Piece, hornbeam and chestnut coppice in Scrubs Wood and 3.6ha (9 acres) of secondary woodland that makes up Spring Wood.

Blake's Wood

Danbury

In Danbury take road towards Little Baddow. Just before Little Baddow turn right. Travel for approx 800m (½ mile)

and car park is on left. (TL773068)
45HA (110 ACRES) SSSI
The National Trust

The Mores

Brentwood

A128 from Brentwood. After 4km (2½ miles) left onto minor road to Bentley. Right after church. Entrance few hundred metres on left. (TQ565967)
16HA (39 ACRES)
The Woodland Trust

Hanningfield Reservoir

Wickford

Turn off B1007 on to Downham Road and turn left onto Hawkswood Road. The visitor centre entrance is just beyond the causeway opposite Crowsheath Lane (TQ725972)

41HA (100 ACRES) SSSI

Essex Wildlife Trust

Closed monday except bank holidays

You don't have to be a bird-lover to enjoy Hanningfield Reservoir. Aside from this vast sanctuary for thousands of birds, there's 40ha (100 acres) of woodland to explore and an excellent visitor centre with fantastic panoramic views.

The reservoir is a Site of Special Scientific Interest (SSSI) where 80,000 swifts, swallows and martins feed in summer but which is best known for its waterfowl. Four hides, one with wheelchair access, provide a vantage point for spotting breeding gadwall, tufted duck and pochard.

About a third of the woodland at the south east end of the reservoir – Well Wood and Hawk's Wood – is ancient woodland with remnants of old hornbeam coppice, currently being re-coppiced. There are some large oak standards with a rich show of bluebells, yellow archangel and stitchwort to enjoy in the spring. Work is also under way to thin out the conifer plantations and open up the rides, glades and ponds.

Hockley Woods

Hockley

From A127 at Rayleigh, take A129 north towards Hockley. Continue onto B1013 Hockley Road, look out for entrance sign on right after golf course. (TQ825913)

130HA (321 ACRES) SSSI

Rochford District Council

The largest ancient woodland site in Essex, Hockley Woods is home to the rare heath fritillary butterfly, reintroduced to the site in 1987 – try spotting one in June and July.

Great for youngsters, with a play area close to a large car park, the woodland features a variety of trees – including the rare wild service tree – and signs of an interesting history. Earthbanks in and around the wood hint at its great age.

Some of the wood's large oaks were battered into interesting shapes by the storms of 1987. Also present are sweet

above:
Hockley Woods

chestnut, birch and hornbeam – or look around the ponds, marshes and stream edges for willow and hazel. Wood anemone, wood spurge and cow-wheat whose yellow flowers persist right through the summer.

There is a wide, surfaced boundary walk but it descends a hill which wheelchair users might find too steep. Parts of the wood get muddy in wet weather so it's a good idea to take wellingtons.

Pound Wood

Thundersley

Turn south off A127 onto A129 and then left onto Daws Heath road at mini roundabout. Bear left to continue on Daws Heath road which becomes Bramble road. Wood is on left.

(TQ816858)

22HA (55 ACRES)

Essex Wildlife Trust

Belfairs Park and Belfairs Nature Reserve

Southend-On-Sea

From A127 take road to Leigh. Traffic lights at T-junction turn right into Eastwood Road. Look out for old green 'Belfairs Park' sign on left and turn right opposite this on track signposted 'Riding School for Disabled' and Golf Club. (TQ820870; TQ830870)

73HA (180 ACRES) SSSI

Southend-on-Sea Borough Council

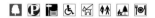

It can take a little determination to get into Belfairs Park. There is no immediately obvious entrance to the wood, which is dissected by the local golf course, although once in you can enjoy guided walks from April to October.

Populated by some very tame squirrels, the woodland – mainly hornbeam, oak, birch and sweet chestnut – is rimmed by a riding track while a separate nature reserve is fenced off but accessible through a gated entrance.

Here the atmosphere is very different, almost secret though well-used, with much denser undergrowth and a delight to explore. Coppicing and pollarding has been taking place for centuries and the observant will spot woodbanks dotted here and there, hollows from

gravel extraction and even the small ponds evolved from bomb craters.

Little Haven

Thundersley

Turn south off A127 at Rayleigh Weir on to Rayleigh road (A129) and turn left onto Daws Heath road at the Woodmans pub mini roundabout. Wood is on left hand side. (TQ811889)

37HA (92 ACRES)

Essex Wildlife Trust

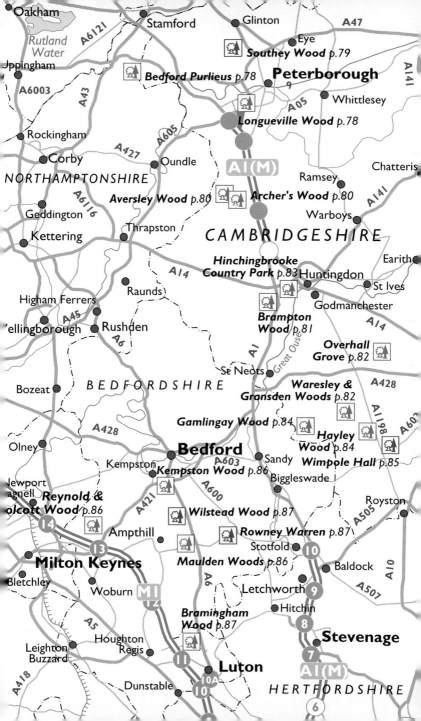

Oakham
Rutland Water
A6121
A6003
A43
Uppingham
Stamford
Glinton
A47
Eye
Southey Wood p.79
Peterborough
Whittlesey
A141
Bedford Purlieus p.78
A05
Longueville Wood p.78
A605
Rockingham
A427
Oundle
A1(M)
Ramsey
Chatteris
Corby
NORTHAMPTONSHIRE
A6116
Aversley Wood p.80
Archer's Wood p.80
A141
Warboys
Geddington
Thrapston
CAMBRIDGESHIRE
Earith
Kettering
Raunds
Hinchingbrooke
Country Park p.83
Huntingdon
St Ives
Higham Ferrers
A45
A14
Godmanchester
A14
Wellingborough
A6
Rushden
Brampton
Wood p.81
A1
Great Ouse
Overhall
Grove p.82
Bozeat
B E D F O R D S H I R E
St Neots
Waresley &
Gransden Woods p.82
A428
A198
A603
A428
Olney
Gamlingay Wood p.84
Bedford
A603
Sandy
Hayley
Wood p.84
Wimpole Hall p.85
A602
Kempston
Kempston Wood p.86
Biggleswade
Newport
Pagnell
Reynold &
Wolcott Wood p.86
A421
A600
Wilstead Wood p.87
Royston
14
Ampthill
Rowney Warren p.87
A505
13
Maulden Woods p.86
Stotfold
10
A10
Milton Keynes
Baldock
Bletchley
Woburn
A6
Letchworth
9
A507
M1
Bramingham
Wood p.87
Hitchin
8
Leighton
Buzzard
A5
Houghton
Regis
11
Stevenage
7
10A
Luton
A1(M)
A418
Dunstable
10
H E R T F O R D S H I R E
6

above:
Longueville Wood

Longueville Wood

Peterborough

Follow signs for Orton Longueville from Peterborough ring road. Past Notcutts garden centre on left. Turn right and park on Lady Lodge drive. (TL161964)

8HA (20 ACRES)

The Woodland Trust

Longueville Wood is an unusual wood with a real sense of history, having been planted in the grounds of Orton Longueville Hall during the 19th century.

A walk along the wood's main ride is almost like walking back through time for the Lord of the Manor collected exotic trees while his wife had a passion for wild flowers. Wellingtonias planted along the main avenue have grown very tall, lending a very grand feel to the main surfaced ride.

The woodland is mixed conifers and broadleaves – beech, sycamore, large false acacia, swamp cypress, large oak pollard and holly. Winter aconite and snowdrops are the first flowers to show, followed by bluebells and wild garlic.

To the east is a large pond with great crested newts. Access is via a wide track, though sections get muddy in wet weather.

Bedford Purlieus

Peterborough or Stamford

From A1 take A47 west towards Leicester. After approx 3km (2 miles) turn left at 'farm access' sign. Keep going until you see Forestry Commission sign. (TL034997)

208HA (514 ACRES) SSSI
Forestry Commission

It's thought that Bedford Purlieus, an ancient woodland remnant of the Royal Forest of Rockingham, sustains a greater variety of plants than any other wood in the country.

In total, some 462 different species of wild flowers, shrubs and trees can be found on this easily navigated site – including the rare large-leaved lime and wild service tree.

The site is made up of a mixture of coppice and high forest – including oak and beech, birch and some conifers – with pockets of limestone grassland.

Thanks to a ride management and scrub clearance programme, the butterfly population is thriving and you might spot white admirals and grizzled skippers among the wild flowers, which include yellow Star-of-Bethlehem and columbine.

Rides are wide, making it easy to walk around but there is no board or leaflet so visitors must rely on instinct to get around the wood. Public footpaths, however, are signed.

Southey Wood

Peterborough
Located on minor road between villages of Upton and Ufford, 11km (7 miles) west of Peterborough. (TF110025)
69HA (171 ACRES)
Forestry Commission

below:
Archer's Wood (see p.80)

Archer's Wood

Sawtry

Come off A1(M) northbound at Sawtry exit. Take turning to Coppingford, at T-junction turn right. Wood is approx 800m (½ mile) on left. (TL174810)
18HA (44 ACRES)
The Woodland Trust

Parts of Archer's Wood are believed to be remnants of the original British wildwood, a ditch and bank in the northern section is a scheduled ancient monument and, true to its name the wood was a sanctuary for 13th-century highwaymen. Even today you look to the north and imagine a 14th-century Cistercian monastic grange that once stood there.

Flat and easy to access, the site is dominated by oak, ash and field maple and served by a figure-of-eight network of rides so it's great for gentle walks. Be sure to stroll along the main ride to spot the rare and beautiful wild service tree – and look out for foxes, woodpeckers and nuthatches.

Coppicing attracts nesting birds and wild flowers and perhaps the best time to visit is spring when the wood is ablaze with bluebells and alive to the sound of the nightingales.

Aversley Wood

Sawtry

Heading north on A1(M) take Sawtry exit. After 400m (¼ mile) turn left into St Judiths Lane, car park is on bend. (TL158815)
62HA (152 ACRES) SSSI
The Woodland Trust

A woodland gem in England's least-wooded county, expansive, impressive Aversley Wood is well worth the steep trek (sometimes boggy in winter) required to reach it.

Believed to date back to the Ice Age, it is one of Cambridgeshire's largest ancient woodland sites.

Wide rides – open and sunny after years of coppicing – make Aversley special: rich in wild flowers, a magnet for butterflies and a haven for birds such as wrens and warblers. You will see plenty of oak and ash and the occasional rare wild service tree while the shrubs lining the rides can be a picture of colourful flowers and berries.

Once part of a 27km (17-mile) woodland belt in Saxon times, the wood is also mentioned in the Domesday Book. A medieval boundary bank in the south indicates this section was once open field.

above:
Aversley Wood

Brampton Wood

Brampton
South bound on A1 take Huntingdon exit and Brampton Hut roundabout, turn right into Brampton, and right again onto Grafham Road. (TL185698)
132HA (326 ACRES) SSSI
The Wildlife Trust for Bedfordshire, Cambridgeshire, Northamptonshire and Peterborough

There is a very rural feel to Brampton Wood, Cambridgeshire's second largest wood, which boasts an abundance of flowers, including primroses and bluebells as well as wild pears and no fewer than 29 species of butterfly.

It has hazel coppice, blackthorn and stands of conifers, streams and wide rides, which emphasise its size and provide a habitat for 46 different breeding species of bird, including grasshopper warbler, nightingale, spotted flycatcher and woodcock. There are also muntjac and fallow deer populations.

Historically the wood was coppiced but this declined and the largest trees were felled during World War II, since then it has lost much of its coppice structure and attained quite a wild feel. However, the Wildlife Trust has reintroduced coppicing since acquiring the site in 1992.

Most of the site sits on chalky boulder clay (and can get muddy) but there are some flat sections and well-drained valleys.

Overhall Grove

Cambridge or Knapwell
From A14 take road signposted to
Boxworth. Once through Boxworth
turn left at crossroads to Knapwell. On
edge of village turn left down a track to
the church. Park beneath the trees in
front of church. (TL337633)
17HA (42 ACRES) SSSI
**The Wildlife Trust for Bedfordshire,
Cambridgeshire, Northamptonshire
and Peterborough**

Believed to be the County's
largest surviving elm wood
with some of the largest oaks
in Cambridgeshire, Overhall
Grove teems with wildlife –
bats, owls, insects and fungi all
thriving in deadwood habitats.

It also features the red well, a
natural spring that rises in the
Wood.

A moated mound, Overhall
Manor, once stood in the
northern part of the wood.
Occupied in the 11th century it
was in decay by 1283 but the
manor fishponds can still be
seen today and mounds and
hollows survive between the
wood and nearby church.

A programme of coppicing
has been reinstated along the
sometimes muddy paths which
provide routes through northern and southern sections.

Waresley and Gransden Woods

Gamlingay
From St Neots take B1046 towards
Great Gransden. At edge of village take
the small road on right running south
west towards Waresley. About 1.6km (1
mile) down this road there is Waresley
Dean Bridge; drive up concrete track
and park in gravel area. (TL263548)
54HA (134 ACRES) SSSI
**The Wildlife Trust for Bedfordshire,
Cambridgeshire, Northamptonshire
and Peterborough**

Waresley and Gransden Woods
is one of those places you
dream of escaping to – a lovely,
peaceful woodland site with a
real feeling of intimacy, thanks
to its relatively narrow paths.

A stream running through a
small valley between the two
woods adds interest to your
walk – you can follow its route
on the waymarked trail.

Dating back to the
Domesday Book, the woodland
has some coppiced areas – hazel
with big ash and oak trees,
where oxlip and bluebells add
colour and interest in the spring.

A large section of Gransden
Wood was felled in 1929 and
has since been replanted with
beech, hornbeam, cherry and
sycamore but be aware that the
northern section is private.

Hinchingbrooke Country Park

Huntingdon

From Huntingdon on A14, take B1514 exit after Swallow Hotel roundabout, signposted to Brampton. From here Country Park is signposted. (TL222718) 73HA (180 ACRES)

Huntingdonshire District Council

The combination of woodland, lakes and open grassland makes for a great place to enjoy a morning or afternoon out with friends and family, particularly children and less abled people, who are well catered for.

Landmarks include a reconstructed Iron Age farm close to the lake (very popular during special activity weeks as a venue for craft and farming demonstrations) and the attractive natural sculptures that dot the landscape.

The woodland – mainly hornbeam, ash, oak and beech – consists of secondary woodland and some recently planted areas.

It takes 30–90 minutes to tour the site on foot but there is plenty to keep the sporty occupied for longer – including a specially designed mountain bike course, water sports and fishing. It's also possible to camp by prior arrangement.

right:
Hinchingbrooke Country Park

Gamlingay Wood

Gamlingay

From A428 take B1040 to Waresley.
Continue towards Gamlingay and
wood is just before the town on left.
(TL242535)

48HA (119 ACRES) SSSI

**The Wildlife Trust for Bedfordshire,
Cambridgeshire, Northamptonshire
and Peterborough**

Gamlingay Wood is an unusual
mixture of ancient woodland –
notably oak and ash – and
conifers. Home to the rare wild
service tree, it comes into its
own in spring and summer
with a riot of flowers, notably
bluebells and oxlip, confirming
its ancient woodland status.

It takes 60–90 minutes to
cover the easy-to-navigate
wood, where the Wildlife
Trust, owner since 1991, has
been thinning conifers, recop-
picing ash, hazel, field maple
and oaks and managing a sizeable deer population.

Bear in mind that, apart from
a distinctive central dry section
with oaks, birch and bracken,
the wood stands on Gault clay
so wellingtons are a 'must' in
wet weather when it gets very
muddy.

below: *Gamlingay Wood*

Hayley Wood

Gamlingay

From A1198 take B1046 towards Great
Gransden. Before you reach village,
there is a water tower on right. Park on
verge and walk up track (TL294534)

48HA (119 ACRES) SSSI

**The Wildlife Trust for Bedfordshire,
Cambridgeshire, Northamptonshire
and Peterborough**

If you would like to see Hayley
Wood at its best, visit in spring
when the bluebells are in flower
and you can see one of the UK's
largest populations of oxlip, or
listen for the nightingales and
great spotted woodpecker.

All are thriving in this ancient woodland, thanks to a policy of coppicing reintroduced by the Wildlife Trust in 1962, and a visit here helps you picture how all coppice woods would once have looked.

Hayley Wood dates back at least 1,000 years and is still enclosed by the original wood-bank. Ironically, the first wood you encounter is actually secondary woodland – oak, hawthorn, birch and sallow with quite a different 'feel' to the rest of the site, which is classic coppice wood – field maple, ash, hazel coppice set beneath big oak trees.

The wood is served by a waymarked trail but it's not immediately obvious and too muddy for less abled visitors.

conservationists. A programme of tree planting, pond and meadow creation makes it a great place for children. Part of Marston Vale Community Forest, the site is mainly occupied by the predominantly semi-natural ancient woodland of Holcot Wood.

Once managed as a coppice but the practice has been reintro-duced in the western section. The rest of the wood, which has a good network of bridleways and paths, is being allowed to develop naturally.

Old hazel and ash coppice are common but you'll also find oak, field maple, Midland hawthorn and hazel. Early spring displays include early-purple orchid, wood anemone, wood sanicle, yellow archangel, primroses and bluebells.

Reynold and Holcot Wood

Cranfield

Leave M1 at junction 13 and follow A421 to Bedford. Turn off A421 just after passing through the village of Brogborough onto a minor road sign-posted to the Brogborough picnic site where parking is available. (SP955400) 98 HA (242 ACRES)

The Woodland Trust

Reynold Wood is a great place for a visit and is a delight for

Wimpole Hall

Royston

Exit M11 at junction 12 and follow signs to Wimpole on A603. After approx 9.5km (6 miles) turn right, fol-lowing brown National Trust signs to Wimpole Hall. (TL336510) 91HA (225 ACRES)

The National Trust

Kempston Wood

Kempston

From A421. Take Kempston turn, left at first roundabout and left at next round-about toward Wooton. At crossroads go straight ahead to wood end, past pub on right follow road out of wood end towards Kempston west end for 800m (½ mile). (SP995470)

17HA (41 ACRES)

The Woodland Trust

This is an ancient woodland site and an historically impor-tant one, with a ditch and bank as evidence of how it was once split to allow coppice manage-ment of one section with animals allowed to graze beneath the trees in the other.

The woodland is populated with ash, oak and field maple trees with hazel, blackthorn and bramble, and various other species including guelder rose and spindle.

It's also home to the wood-pecker, nuthatch and tree creeper. There's even a good chance you'll spot a muntjac deer during your visit. Spring brings a good show of flowers – among them bluebell, early-purple orchid, wood anemone and wood-sorrel.

Generally the paths are good, some steep sections.

Maulden Woods

Ampthill

Maulden wood accessed from Deadmans Hill layby on A6 adjacent to the wood. (TL073395)

149HA (368 ACRES) SSSI

Forestry Commission

A spacious ride leading from the entrance to Maulden Wood helps create the illusion that this diverse and interesting site is larger than it really is.

Designated a Site of Special Scientific Interest (SSSI) because the clay and sand soil gives a distinctive wood pattern, it's a pleasant area to tour – a mixture of broadleaved woodland, locally rare acidic grasslands and conifer plantations.

Close to one of the benches within the wood is a fine exam-ple of the rare wild service tree though most of the broadleaves are focused on the ride edges while behind them are dense blocks of conifers. One 20-year-old Christmas tree crop is being removed to help restore a corri-dor of acidic grassland that runs through the wood. This will connect up two fragmented heathland areas that have been designated SSSI.

Look out too for art and sculptures in the wood, created last year by an artist in residence.

Bramingham Wood

Luton

From centre of Luton take A6 towards Bedford. Near outskirts of Luton turn left into Icknield Way. Take right fork after about 800m (½ mile). Turn right at roundabout into Northwell Drive, turn right again at the next roundabout into Lygetun Drive. (TL069259)

18HA (45 ACRES)

The Woodland Trust

Bramingham Wood is an ancient woodland sanctuary in a very urban environment, shielded by oak, ash and field maples.

An acre of the site is recopiced each year (the produce is sold locally), producing open areas that attract butterflies such as peacock, red admiral and occasionally speckled wood, brimstone and comma.

Birds include the tawny owl, great spotted woodpecker, nuthatch, sparrowhawk, woodcock and in the winter, yellow hammers, reed buntings and finches. Wood mice, voles, moles and shrews also inhabit the wood. The wood is home to several native fungi species found nowhere else in Britain, among them a species discovered in 1986. Floral delights include snowdrops, bluebells, red campion, wood anemone and enchanter's nightshade.

Wilstead Wood

Shefford or Kempston

Wilstead village is to east of A6, south of Bedford. Just past 'White Lodge' there are some black wrought iron gates set back off road with Haynes Park RSPB sign on. Park here and go round the gates that mark the start of the carriageway which will lead you up to the wood (10–15 min walk). (TL073429)

63HA (156 ACRES)

Forestry Commission

Rowney Warren

Shefford

Rowney Warren is in Sandy lane, off the A600 (signposted Chicksands). (TL124403)

71HA (176 ACRES)

Forestry Commission

Marston Vale Community Forest

The Forest of Marston Vale covers over 160km^2 (61 sq. miles) in the heart of Bedfordshire. It is a place where local people are discovering and enjoying the countryside, some for the first time. The vision for the future of the Forest is to recreate a natural landscape for the next generation.

Further Information

The Woodland Trust

Trees and forests are crucial to life on our planet. They generate oxygen, play host to a spectacular variety of wildlife and provide us with raw materials and shelter. They offer us tranquillity, inspire us and refresh our souls.

Founded in 1972, the Woodland Trust is now the UK's leading woodland conservation charity. By acquiring sites and campaigning for woodland it aims to conserve, restore and re-establish native woodland to its former glory. The Trust now owns and cares for over 1,000 woods throughout the UK.

The Woodland Trust wants to see:

* no further loss of ancient woodland

* the variety of woodland wildlife restored and improved

* an increase in new native woodland

* an increase in people's awareness and enjoyment of woodland

The Woodland Trust has over 100,000 members who share this vision. It only costs £2.50 a month to join but your support would be of great help in ensuring the survival of Britain's magnificent ancient woodland heritage. For every new member, the Trust can care for approximately another half acre. For details of how to join the Woodland Trust please ring FREEPHONE 0800 026 9650 or visit the website at www.woodland-trust.org.uk.

If you have enjoyed the woods in this book please consider leaving a legacy to the Woodland Trust. Legacies of all sizes play an invaluable role in helping the Trust to create new woodland and secure precious ancient woodland threatened by development and destruction. For further information please call 01476 581129.

Public Transport

Each entry gives a brief description of location, nearest town and a grid reference. Traveline provides impartial journey planning information about all public transport services by ringing 0870 608 2608 (minicom 0870 241 2216) (calls charged at national rates). For information about the Sustrans National Cycle Network ring 0117 929 0888.

Useful Contacts

The Forestry Commission, 0131 334 3047, www.forestry.gov.uk

The National Trust, 020 7222 9251, www.nationaltrust.org.uk

The Wildlife Trusts, 0870 036 7711, www.wildlifetrusts.org

RSPB, 01767 680551, www.rspb.org.uk

The Royal Forestry Society, 01442 822028, www.rfs.org.uk

The Woodland Trust, 01476 581111, www.woodland-trust.org.uk